HEAVE

Karen Oppenheim

BALBOA.
PRESS
A DIVISION OF HAY HOUSE

Balboa Press books may be ordered through booksellers or by contacting:

Balboa Press
A Division of Hay House
1663 Liberty Drive
Bloomington, IN 47403
www.balboapress.com
1 (877) 407-4847

ISBN: 978-1-5043-9119-1 (sc)
ISBN: 978-1-5043-9120-7 (e)

Library of Congress Control Number: 2017917193

Print information available on the last page.

Balboa Press rev. date: 02/19/2018

Heave

The low buzz of the old neon sign coming on was backup for a cricket band that broke into song every evening this time of year. The amped-up insects took five as I stepped out my screen door into the pink glow of fuchsia letters spelling "Heave." Years ago the "n" at the end had gone dark, signifying a drastic drop of business for this once run-down motel that, thanks to the Interstate, is located on a road now less traveled by. A blinking arrow below the letters pulsated toward what had been the office.

I could see the Big Dipper. And there was a slight breeze, as if the desert let out a long sigh before it settled down after a scorching June day to let the cooler minds of its nocturnal inhabitants take watch. Somewhere in the Santa Rosa Mountains a coyote called out.

"That you, Maebeth?" It was Lily Jackson cooling off on a lawn chair perched on her patio, one down from mine, with her mutt, Beau, curled up at her feet and the dreamy voice of Nat King Cole escaping through her screen door. Lily, as misnamed as the motel Heaven, was the tallest, skinniest African American woman I had ever seen. All 6'2" of her arrived in the Palm Springs area three years earlier from Savannah, with Beau riding shotgun and enough faux Louis Vuitton luggage for a booth at the Street Fair. Lily buried her husband of 35 years and hours after the funeral, piled what she cared about in her '85 white Cadillac and headed west. Life with Benjamin had never been easy, but he had given her two fine boys, Henry and Dennis.

About the time Benny took sick a few years back, Lily began to campaign

1

for a unit. She had heard about Heave from her old friend Charlotte—Charo to us, whose only daughter, Sarah, who, like me, had been one of the original residents, had succumbed to breast cancer.

"Heat's a bitch, isn't it, Lily?" I said as I fanned myself with a six-month-old issue of *Nutrition Action*.

"You got that right. Sit yourself down and let me fetch you a cold Beck's."

Lily brushed a springy salt and pepper strand of hair behind her ear and wound out of her webbed aluminum chair like a rattler. Old Beau was lifting his head, which took all the effort he could muster, when all three of us saw him walking down the two-lane highway.

Hmmm. Little toasty for a midnight stroll.

It was rare to see someone this late in the evening hoofing it in the middle of the desert. I stayed put in my chair as the stranger approached. I could see he was tall and didn't seem to be in any great hurry. A cap prevented me from getting a good look at his face.

"Let me do the talking, Lily."

She nodded.

"You lost something, Mister?"

"Just some pride and possibly the radiator on my pickup," he said as he removed his Lakers cap. "Name's Luke. Luke Washington. I was on my way to LA when I got sidetracked looking for a bite to eat and got off on a wrong exit. You wouldn't know if there's an extra room at this motel where I could get some rest and try my luck tomorrow with a garage?"

"Why this ain't no motel, Mr. Luke. This here our home," Lily said, slipping into her lazy southern dialect, which always seems to happen whenever she sees a good-looking man.

The Mob Boss
Maebeth

*T*he idea for Heave was mine. I wanted a place for older broads who, although aware of their years, weren't even close to being dead. Ladies who sought independence and needed a place to flourish in the company of like souls. The idea took shape when I spotted a classified ad in The Desert Sun under "Business Opportunities." The ad suggested the former Heaven was a fixer-upper waiting for the right entrepreneur. The motel had 16 units, a big office, a neglected pool in the back, a string of cement-floor front patios and a lot of Midcentury Desert Modern panache that seemed to be the trend these post-Rat Pack days.

I rounded up seven of my friends and family who wanted in. We pooled our money, bought the place, had walls removed so each of us had the equivalent of two units with a good–sized living room, bedroom, bath and galley kitchen that had its own back door leading to the pool. We fixed up the old motel office and named it Monistat 1. This was our Presidential Suite for when family and friends stayed over. In the back we spruced up the pool and built a cutting-edge fitness center and laundry room with lots of comfortable seating and card tables. This central meeting space was named The Way of the Cross. A few of the Catholics initially balked but came around after a while.

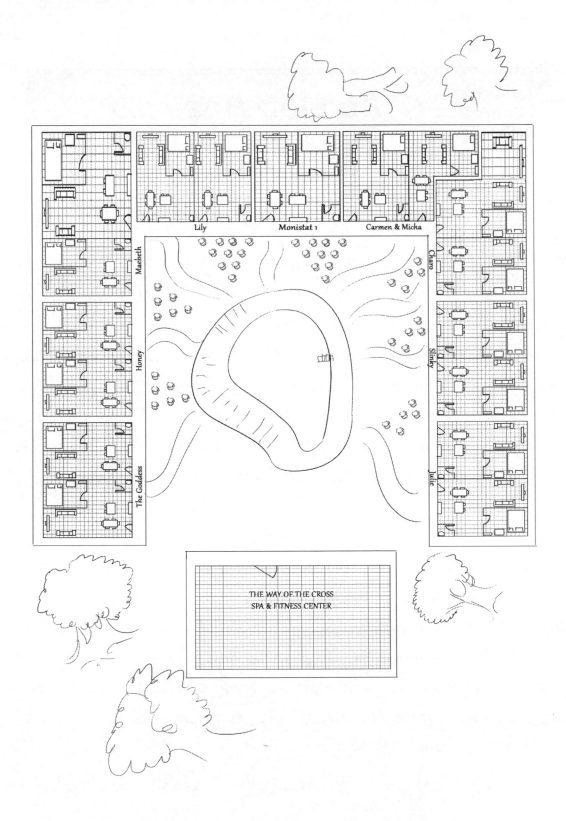

Lily

Monistat 1

Carmen & Micha

Maebeth

Charo

Honey

Slinky

The Goddess

Julie

THE WAY OF THE CROSS
SPA & FITNESS CENTER

Introductions

I extended my hand. "I'm Maebeth Caletti. And this is Lily, Lily Jackson. We live here. Some of us got together a few years back, renovated this Bellagio knockoff and figured there'd be safety in numbers. There are eight of us—well, nine actually—my sister Carmen has a roommate. Used to be a motel called Heaven but the "n" dropped off and Heave really says it all. Did I mention that we're all skilled in martial arts?"

Luke smiled.

"Well, Miz Caletti, could you please tell me where the nearest motel or closest town might be? I doubt very much if I could rouse AAA at this hour."

"Call me Maebeth. If you're not a serial killer or wanted rapist, we could put you up in what was once the motel office. We call it Monistat 1. It's not the Ritz, but it's clean and there's a bedroom, bathroom and kitchenette. We use it when any of our friends or kids drop in. Otherwise, the nearest town is Thermal and there isn't much there except for a feed and hardware store, gas station, Mexican restaurant and Circle K. It's a few miles up the road."

Luke smiled and appeared to be sizing me up.

I'm no Raquel Welch, but I'm not Ugly Betty either.

It's been said that I have male energy—whatever that means. My dark brown hair is thick, curly and always losing a battle with armies of tortoise combs. I'm about 5'5" so I had to shelve the modeling route.

Tonight I was not exactly dressed for success in a sleeveless red tank with white letters across my average chest that read *SEE YOU'VE MET THE*

5

TWINS and white cotton shorts along with white leather sandals that I hoped complimented my tan 58-year-old runner's legs.

My only claim to femininity was bright red polish on my toes and my grandmother's exquisite gold and ruby drop earrings that I never take off. Everyone says the two of us could have been twins, which I take as the highest of compliments because my saint of a grandmother had been famous for never needing much makeup, wearing these antique earrings and sporting a twinkle in her almond-shaped brown eyes.

She also spent a large part of her life praying to St. Anthony, swore only in Italian and cooked from scratch, so we weren't totally alike.

Lily started to fidget, brushing strands of hair off her forehead, batting away imaginary mosquitoes. She was wearing a bright red muumuu that billowed like a windsock when she moved and shocking pink flip flops.

Luke grinned.

"Much obliged Maebeth, Monistat 1 sounds perfect and I can assure you that the only time I've done was overnight long ago as a Freedom Rider in Jackson, Mississippi. If you ladies will excuse me, I'll head back to my truck, which is only about a mile down the road, and get my things."

"We'll be here," I said. "Oiling our firearms. We do this most evenings when we're not honing our waterboarding techniques."

Luke shook his head, put his Lakers cap back on and stepped off the porch. He was about 6'3" and I guessed early 60s but still muscular. His skin was the color of a new penny and not as black as Lily's. He had on khaki pants and a white golf shirt, expensive loafers, no socks.

Note to Maebeth: Look up the dress code for rapists and serial killers.

As we watched him head back down the road, Lily said, "Maebeth, you don't know squat about that man. What you thinkin', girl?"

I got up from the chair and followed Lily into her unit. The screen door slammed behind us. It was like stepping back into the '60s with red-beaded curtains going into the galley kitchen, crushed velvet gold pillows on a lime green sofa, fringed throws, a lava lamp.

"Lily, the man seems legit and he's in trouble. Hang loose."

"Goddamn," Lily screamed slapping her skinny thigh, "Heee mine."

"Lily, cut the Aunt Jemima crap." Lily has a master's degree from Howard University and taught expository writing at a college in the south for 27 years.

When Sarah's unit became available, I liked what I heard about Lily and voted her in sight unseen on the strong recommendation of 85-year-old Charo, Heave's oldest resident. Charo has a primo end unit like mine, only she has extensively renovated it and now has the largest kitchen in the place for which all of our stomachs are eternally grateful.

The house rule was that for whatever reason one opted out, the unit became the possession of the remaining residents who were free to vote in whomever they agreed upon. Even though I have more invested in the place than anyone else, we all have one vote when it comes to inviting someone new in and we split the proceeds evenly from a resale. In addition, we have a tenants-in-common arrangement and owners pay a monthly fee to ensure that the common grounds are kept up and that there is a reserve for any extraordinary expenses.

I became part of the free agent nation in my late 50s and make money writing brochures, TV commercials, annual reports, billboards—the whole marketing enchilada. Truth is, I'm good at it; it leaves me enough time for play, and I'd rather stick a pencil in my ear than work for anyone else at this point. Black pant suits and sensible low heels are no longer part of my wardrobe.

None of us at Heave is formally attached, but there are still a few of us who are getting it on a regular basis. All of us have enough baggage to fill a boxcar. The deaths, marriages, children, jobs, achievements and bombshells have shaped us like old slippers. Our ages range from mid-50s to mid-80s and our collective mantra is "freedom is power." There are no Jell-O mold salads, bingo games or activity directors in sight and that's the way we plan to keep it. Screw water aerobics.

We left the screen door open and in walked Mr. Silverman.

"Who let the cat in?" Lily said while reaching into the refrigerator for three cold beers.

Mr. Silverman, my huge gray former stray, can be intimidating as hell, but he is the sweetest thing in the universe with a beating heart.

"Maebeth, that damn cat is lookin' to pee all over my antiques. Would you please ask him to return to his natural environment?"

"Oh, for crissakes Lily, Silverman isn't marking a thing. He has more class than that," I said as I stroked the big guy behind the ears.

There was a slight rap on the screen door and the sound of a throat clearing.

It's Luke, duffel in one hand, a book in the other.

"That'd be the Duke, Duke, Duke, Duke of Earl," Lily sang.

The Wordsmith
Lily Jackson

The beauty, the rhythm of Black English is what I would love to have taught my college students during my day. Back then it was frowned upon as nothing more than a collection of slang and bad grammar, but today it be (ha, ha) considered okay by some of the more well-known linguists.

I get a kick out of my boys and their friends, goofin' and riffin'. It's like a symphony to me.

I give Maebeth a hard time when I slip into Black English. She knows it means I'm up to somethin' and she be correct. Ha, ha.

When Benny got sick and passed, I realized that there was nothin' in Savannah for me. My boys were established, had their own lives and I didn't want to be a burden. So, I answered the call of Heave, loaded up my old Caddy and my mutt, Beau, and I headed west.

I love it here at Heave. I thank my BFF Charo for telling me about this wonderful way to grow old. Regardless of what that ratty old neon sign reads, Heave is truly heaven.

Getting Acquainted

It was late. Luke, Lily and I were working on our second beer. Lily made a meatloaf, lettuce and hot mustard sandwich on 7-grain bread for Luke. The meatloaf was leftover from one of Charo's finer efforts.

Lily changed the CD to Billie Holiday who was singing "Lover Man Oh Where Can You Be."

Beau was showing his parts to the stars, legs in the air and snoring. Mr. Silverman had begun his night shift and departed into the desert.

Luke told us he was semi-retired, doing a little private investigative work after a long stint with the National Security Agency.

"So how long were you in the NSA, Luke?" I asked.

"Too long, Maebeth. Not much I can really talk about or actually want to remember. Now, I'm doing PI work and thanks to some good investments, can pretty well do what I want, when I want. I'm not wealthy, but I'll never need to wear a clearance badge anymore or kiss up to 'the man.'"

"Isn't that kind of quiet after all that undercover stuff?" Lily asked.

"I needed things to slow down, Lily. To settle. After literally being in a gun site for so long, you stop appreciating some of the better things in life. Take this fine night for example, and this fascinating company, and that mighty wonderful sandwich."

"Compliments of Charo Blake," Lily said, smoothing out her muumuu and pointing palm up to the end unit. "Lawdy, she's the gourmet around here. It's a wonder we're all not clockin' in at 175 pounds. Maybe you'll have a chance to meet her tomorrow before you take off."

"Wouldn't mind havin' that meatloaf recipe, Lily. Think Miz Charo might share her secret?"

"You're starting to sound like you'd fit right in here," I said, trying my damnedest not to stare. "All of us girls are looking to take it a day at a time and make each day the richest possible. Someone that enraptured by meatloaf is in the moment, I'd say."

"I know that sounds corny," Lily said. She had dropped the ghetto gab after the second beer. "But it's so true. I knew I was headed here even before Benny, my husband, passed on. Heave sounded just like what I'd been waiting for all my life. A chance to belong, to be part of something, to be myself and be with others who 'got it.'"

"How about you, Maebeth? What brought you to this quiet place?" Luke asked.

I had my feet propped up on the patio rail and after a couple beers was looking forward to forced sex with Luke.

"Luke, I've been looking for and taking note of magic moments all my life. Remember back in the '60s when you danced so close you held your breath. When The Four Lads would turn you to mush and your dance partner would wind your arm behind you. Like a pancake wouldn't fit between the two of you. And you hardly traveled two feet on the dance floor.

"Or, when you'd be sitting on the hood of a car on a hot summer night. A whistle of a train in the distance while you're watching the local boys play baseball under the lights, hearing the crack of a homerun on a wooden bat, looking up at the stars and wondering where you'd be in 10 years.

"Well, the irony was that those were the magic moments, not where you'd be in the next 10 years. So, I've tried to dedicate myself to spotting those moments and appreciating them for what they are. That's why Heave seems so right. None of us have given up. We've got our radar up for the good times, knowing full well how short this journey is. Ahhh shit, well, you asked." I blushed at revealing so much. "Christ, I sound like Oprah."

Luke held my eyes with a long steady gaze. Nothing stirred. The universe was holding its breath and we both knew it.

Where's the fucking cricket band when you need it?

Billie Holiday was now singing "Crazy He Calls Me." Lily was the first to break the spell. "I have to drag Beau in and get my beauty sleep. It's late. Come on Beau," she said as she nudged his tummy with her foot, all the while trying to hide a coy smile.

Beau got up, stretched his 45 pounds, gave a snort and headed out to a bush to lift his leg.

"Well," I said smoothing my shorts, suppressing a beer belch and tucking an errant curl back into a comb, "Let's show you Monistat 1 and get you settled."

Luke grabbed his duffel and book and followed me to the office, which was adjacent to my sister Carmen Carlotta's unit.

"What are you reading?" I asked.

"Would you believe it's *Lonesome Dove*? Never had time for novels before, but this book proves just how wrong I was. Do you read much, Maebeth?"

"Hmmm, oh yeah."

Why am I so nervous?

I opened the door and turned on the overhead light. The aroma of lavender potpourri greeted us. The office done in its original knotty pine has a clubby feel to it. The front counter and key rack are still in place, but now the counter is stacked with back issues of *Bazaar, Vogue and Elle*. Tucked in the corner is a queen-size canopy bed with an eyelet bedskirt and white linens trimmed in lace with a light pink matlisse. A Shabby Chic nightstand with a fake Tiffany lamp and dresser with a Smart TV on top complete the look. There is also a tiny galley kitchen done in French Country and a full bath at the other end of the room.

Luke burst out laughing. "Thanks, Maebeth, I think I'll just have a spot of tea, put on some moisture cream and my pink hairnet and leaf through *Vogue* before I turn in."

"I spotted you for a wiseass the moment your chinos hit the chair. Lily's two boys have that same attitude when they visit. This room breaks them up. I'll never understand men. Anyone who thinks burping and farting are hilarious leaves me cold."

"Sorry, Maebeth," Luke said holding one side to keep from erupting all over again. "Guess it's too many beers. And come on, did I break up when you told me the name of this suite? I haven't felt this relaxed in years."

"Well, there are clean towels in the cabinet by the bathroom sink. And you've got Netflix if you want to catch a flick."

"Maebeth," Luke said, in what sounded like a stage whisper, "thank you very much." He extended his hand very slowly and looked hard at me.

I took his hand lightly in mine and looked at him a little too long. Everything seemed as if it had been too long. Too long that a handsome man stopped by—too long since I felt this alive.

"Have a good night's sleep," I said, but it didn't sound as if it was my voice.

My God, I don't even know this man. He's black. I'm unlucky in love. What am I thinking?

Wake Up!

I heard a car door slam, someone blurt "fuck it," and high heels clicking past my bedroom window. I reached over to check the clock on the nightstand. The green glow of the digital numbers read 2:48 a.m. Then there was a soft rapping at my door.

"Maebeth, you sleeping? You awake Maebeth?"

I got up, tugged my oversized tee down past my butt and opened the door.

"No, Honey, I had to get up to answer the door, come on in," I said through pinched lips.

Honey Dean is a torch singer. She just turned 61 but looks more like 48. She has spiky blonde hair, is about 5'8" and still wears a bikini to the pool out back. She watches what she eats, exercises most mornings with an old Karen Voight video and has been an entertainer her entire life. She still maintains a teenager's view of romance, is always falling in white hot love and has a string of bad marriages and memories to prove it.

Honey's idea of celibacy is to live at Heave with a bunch of women, but there is always a fancy car or motorcycle parked outside her unit. She is a dear friend, but we have little in common.

Tonight she was wearing a long, sleek, red dress, cut low with tiny sequined spaghetti straps that matched dangly rhinestone earrings that grazed her shoulders. She was singing at a nightclub in Palm Springs three nights a week. Not much money, but a nice gig to have and it keeps her in front of an audience, which is where she wants to be most in life. Her shoes are towering,

14

spiky, silver-strapped sandals and she was dragging a black-fringed shawl on the floor.

As we were standing at the door, Mr. Silverman ambled in, rubbing the side of my right leg like he owned it. I reached down behind his ears, leaned over, and said, "You my big man, are you in for the night with mama?"

"I got trouble, Maebeth," Honey choked out, a tear running down her cheek, "I think Lenny's looking for me."

"Oh, no, not that dickweed Lenny again."

Lenny was husband #4 and had been passionately in love with her up until the honeymoon when he just as passionately broke her nose and caused her to get eight stitches over her left eyebrow.

Honey had chosen a lacy thong as part of her bridal trousseau and as they were getting ready to hop on the waterbed at the Flamingo Hotel in Vegas, something snapped and it wasn't the elastic in her thong.

Lenny screamed at what a whore she was dressing like that and he'd fix it so no one would look at her again. That marriage lasted two months. It was three years ago and during that time she hadn't heard from him, but had heard that he was involved with some bad people and was doing some post-grad work in Lancaster as a guest of the California state prison system. The prison is in the Mohave Desert about 40 miles northeast of Los Angeles.

"I was just finishing my set tonight and out of nowhere this guy comes up to me and says that Lenny sends his regards," Honey said.

"That's it?"

"Isn't it enough?" Honey sobbed, her mascara making tracks down her cheeks. "You know he wants me dead."

I put water in two mugs, added some Zen tea, and stuck them in the microwave.

"Jesus, Honey."

The bell chimed, the tea was ready. I sat the mugs on the kitchen table and pulled up a chair.

Tonight Honey looked her age. She sipped her tea and grabbed my hand that was resting on the Formica tabletop. "You are the best friend anyone would ever want, Maebeth Caletti. I so needed to talk to you."

"Sip your Zen, calm down and let's see what we need to do tomorrow about that jerk Lenny. Oh, and we've got protection, tonight. A man by the name of Luke Washington had his truck break down and we're putting him up in Monistat 1 until he can get on his way. So, if you see Morgan Freeman walking by in the morning, don't slug him with a skillet or seduce him. It's okay."

"So he's hot!" Honey said, smoothing her long red dress and Indian-combing her spiked blonde hair with splayed fingers.

"Honey, I'm whacked. Let's call it a night. You'll meet The Hulk in the morning and we'll figure out this Lenny thing," I said as I stood to clear the mugs from the table.

The Siren

Honey Dean

Sometimes I could just bitch-slap a few of these old heifers. Don't think I don't catch Maebeth's sister, Carmen, shooting me the stink eye now and again.

Truth is, I'm misunderstood. My voice is my God-given instrument that has been my bread-n-butter and gotten me recognition. I've been around the block a few times, but have never given up on making it big time. It just takes one Hollywood bigshot to catch my set and see my range. I've still got it! Still turn heads. Do you think this figure is just luck? Not so, it takes work and I've probably spent more time at The Way of the Cross than all of those Golden Girls put together.

Men have been my downfall. I love, love, love them all. Problem is I always pick the wrong ones. They seem cool at first, but when they discover there's a brain inside this gorgeous body, well, that's all folks.

Being smart, beautiful and talented is a double-edged sword, or should it be triple-bladed, maybe like an American Red Cross pocket knife? I dunno.

Getting a Start on the Day

Mornings in the desert are something to behold. There is no such thing as a bad one. Each dawn the mountains take on a soft pink hue as the sun begins to crawl up into a lip gloss sky.

The sign had been off since first light. Heave always looks a little rough in the morning light, but I am proud how we fixed her up. It's like a little bit of Tuscany dropped into the desert. The stucco has been sponged with a dull gold leaving all the chips and flaws which adds to the character. Each tenant chose to paint her front door a different color and there's no homeowner rule on what kind of furniture goes on the huge front patio that winds its way around the property. There is a hammock, a glider, lawn and rocking chairs and it all seems to work in some thrown together way.

The old motel is just off the now seldom used highway with the neon sign close to the road. Right across from Heave is a huge date grove and next to it an avocado field.

But it's the back of Heave that is a fairyland. Besides the completely redone pool, there's a whirlpool spa along with two gold and white striped cabanas, chaises, a large gas grill, canopied bar and picnic table. The landscaping is desert with low maintenance native plants, but clay pots of red and white geraniums during the cooler months are scattered around the motel's front and back perimeter and are all thanks to my sister Carmen's green thumb.

Today's outfit is ratty old denim running shorts and a navy tank top with *God Bless This Hot Mess* written in rhinestones across the front. I went out my back door to the pool and started to pick up a few plastic glasses that had been left out overnight.

I could smell eggs, bacon and biscuits coming from Charo's back screen door. I willed myself to head down the highway for my morning run. It was about 5:30 a.m. and would still be pleasant for another few hours before the heat shows the desert who's boss.

I wanted to get back before Luke took off. And, I needed to check on Honey first thing. I had never seen her so distraught and in truth, Lenny is one scary dude and we all need to pay attention to this ticking timebomb.

I jogged down to The Crossings where there is a general store with a small café attached and a gas pump out front. It's about two miles south of Heave and I clipped along at a good pace. Running is how I empty my mind. Nothing but the moment matters.

As I pulled up to The Crossings, I slowed my pace.

Sweat was dripping down my temples and my hair must have looked like Einstein's. Catching my breath, I bent over and rested my hands on my knees as I approached the café's front door. I was still in this position when the door opened and two New Balance running shoes with blue stripes pulled up in front of me.

"Morning Maebeth," Luke said. "I might have guessed you'd be out here trying to get a jump on the day."

"Why Mr. Washington," I said. "How was your evening in Monistat 1? Pleasant, I do hope. Any housekeeping hints picked up from those periodicals?"

"I did read a great article on how to ward off hot flashes. Never knew you ladies had to put up with such stuff."

"It's just another reason why we live longer, Luke. Release all the poison on our men, wait for them to die, take their money and split."

"Care if I head back with you, Maebeth? Always more incentive to keep a good pace when a beautiful woman is running next to me."

"Suit yourself, hot stuff, but let me get a bottle of water first."

This guy is so easy to be around. God, what a body! Did he say "beautiful"?

Good Morning

"Maebeth, what you doin' out there? Are you chasing that handsome man or runnin' from him?" It was Charo out on her patio, sitting on her glider reading the *Los Angeles Times* as we trotted up to Heave.

"Charo, meet Luke Washington. He appeared here last night," I said.

"So Lily told me," Charo said. "I don't suppose either of you kids would be interested in some breakfast. Got some scrambled eggs, bacon, homemade biscuits, apple butter and fresh-squeezed orange juice on the menu."

"Luke, is that sweat or saliva coming out of the sides of your mouth?" I asked.

"Woman, you do have a way with words. Why Miz Charo, I would be honored to have breakfast with you, but first I'd like to take a quick shower."

"Me too, Charo. I'll be over shortly," I said.

Luke grinned.

"A man could certainly get accustomed to this fine company. Are all you ladies so good looking and talented?"

"You've only met three of us. And we are the pick of the litter, buster. At this very moment you are at the top of the bell curve."

I walked past Lily's heading toward my unit when I heard her call out. Still in her nightgown, she was holding a mug of coffee and leaning against her screen door. Beau was already taking his first siesta of the day on the porch.

"You two done it yet?" Lily asked.

I put my hands on me hips and glared.

"Jesus, Lily, he'll hear you. And no, we have more of a cerebral relationship than anything else."

"My nose says Charo's cookin'," Lily said.

"Yep, see you over there. Have you seen Honey this morning?"

"Honey, nobody sees Honey anymore in the morning. That girl lives in another world. Did she bother you last night or was it The Goddess' turn?"

"Lily, I'll catch up with you at Charo's. I need to wash my hair and take a quick shower."

When, I got back home, the phone was ringing. It was The Goddess who lives in #8 on the other side of Honey.

The Goddess is gorgeous with perfect creamy skin, perfect long blonde hair, perfect teeth, perfect figure and a perfect attitude. It's tough to be queen, but she does it well. She is the youngest in the group. At 54, it is pretty early for her to be living at Heave, but it's what she wants. The Goddess' unit is the only one with a screened in side porch. It is here that she entertains, often near naked, in her hammock that is big enough to accommodate three adults and sometimes does. She is the only one of us who still goes off to work each day. The Goddess understands men, but enjoys the company of her girlfriends whom she is wise enough to trust a lot more than her suitors.

"Maebeth, what's with Honey?" The Goddess asked. "I was just leaving for work and walked by #6 and her door was wide open and she wasn't in there. Her car is still here, but it's odd that she would leave the door open. Her purse is still inside on the dining room table. Nothing looks disturbed. It's just that she's nowhere in sight. I'm coming over."

The Goddess was wearing a light gray Armani pantsuit with a pink silk camisole. She had on low-heel black pumps and her hair was in a tight knot at her nape. She looked nothing like the wild creature she really is and that suits everyone at Merrill Lynch just fine. The Goddess is a stockbroker and has been generous with suggestions that paid off quite handsomely for some of the Heave residents.

"Let's not panic," I said. "Honey was a little upset last night and this might be a carryover. She's gotta be around here someplace."

"Well, call me if there's a problem," The Goddess said as she opened the door of her black BMW. The car was also perfect. Perfectly clean. Perfectly everything.

The Goddess

Let's Leave it at That

To paraphrase the song, I've come through the desert as a girl with no name.

Actually, that's not totally true—I am The Goddess. When my friends at Heave first laid that name on me, I thought they were referring to salad dressing. Later I would learn that they just enjoy thinking I'm perfect.

Yes, I enjoy nice clothes, cars and lots of cash, but isn't there more to life than that? Of course there is. There are boys and they are fabulous to play with. They make me feel young and carefree and that's something after 10-hour days watching the stock market.

As the youngest resident of Heave, friends outside our coven questioned why I would want to be part of an older group of girls at such a young age.

I tell them I'm a connoisseur of all things fine. So a touch of heaven on earth suits me just fine.

Hmmm, Hmmm Good

I finished my shower and threw on a pair of khaki shorts, a black sleeveless tee that read *COACHELLA* in white block letters and a pair of Born beige sandals. Tied my hair back with a red kerchief and headed down to Charo's.

Luke and Charo were already fast friends. Luke was at the kitchen table with his chair tilted back grinning at me and rubbing his stomach as I came into the room. If food and sex are all men want, Charo was halfway home with Luke.

"Maebeth, I am definitely in love," Luke said sipping his black coffee and winking at Charo.

"And this boy can EAT," Charo said. "Let's get you fixed up, Maebeth."

I put a biscuit and a helping of scrambled eggs on my plate. Charo poured me a glass of orange juice.

"You are damn lucky Luke Washington that it isn't Sunday," I said.

"You be careful, Maebeth," Charo said.

"And why might that be Miz Carlotti?"

"Well, my man, you would be clogging those arteries of yours faster than rush hour on the 501."

I explained to our guest that Sunday was when Charo whipped up Eggs Portugal.

Karen Oppenheim
Eggs Portugal

1 lb. Farmer John Sausage

8 slices white or wheat bread

¾ lb. grated Cheddar cheese

1 4-oz. can sliced mushrooms

2½ cups milk

4 eggs

¾ tsp prepared mustard

1 can Cream of Mushroom soup

½ cup dry vermouth or sherry

Brown sausage; cube bread. Place bread in large casserole dish; divide cheese, mushrooms and sausage over bread. Mix milk, eggs, mustard and dash of salt. Pour over bread and refrigerate overnight. Blend soup and vermouth and pour into casserole. Bake uncovered for 1 hour at 350 degrees.

"While you're sharing recipes, Miz Charo, might I have the one for your meatloaf I tasted last night? Why it had to be the best ever," Luke said.

That's all Charo needed to hear. She ran up to Luke and nearly knocked him off the chair. At 5'1" and 113 lbs. she isn't much of a threat, but she loves the attention and gave him a big wet kiss on the cheek to show her pleasure. Charo is always well-groomed. No matter how hot the temperature, she is always sparkling with makeup, matching earrings and necklace and a pressed pantsuit.

"Why you big charmer you," Charo said. "Would you believe I call that recipe my Best Ever Meatloaf? You must be psychic," she said as she grabbed her tin box of recipes.

Best Ever Meatloaf

2 eggs

2/3 cup milk

2 tsp salt

¼ tsp pepper

3 slices bread, crumbled

1 onion, chopped

½ cup raw carrots, shredded

1 cup cheddar cheese

1½ lbs. ground beef

Topping:

¼ cup brown sugar

¼ cup catsup

1 tbsp prepared mustard

Beat eggs in large bowl. Add milk, salt, pepper and bread. Beat until the bread has disintegrated. Add onion, carrot, cheese and beef. Mix well, form into loaf and place in baking pan. Combine sugar, catsup and mustard. Spread over surface of the loaf. Bake 1 hour at 350 degrees

NOTE: For a change of taste. Substitute ½ cup shredded raw potatoes for the carrot. Good!

Paging Ms. Dean

"Well, if you girls will excuse me," I said as I carried my dishes to the sink. I was still worried about Honey. Something was off. I thanked Charo for breakfast and headed toward the front door. Luke must have sensed my mood because he got up and followed me.

"Something wrong Maebeth?"

I explained my concern about Honey and replayed last evening's conversation. Luke seemed to change right before my eyes. His eyes darkened, his body straightened, he cleared his throat and asked if we could go someplace private because he had something that needed discussing.

We went back to my unit and I held the screen door open for him and gestured toward my denim slipcovered couch. Luke sat down, put his elbows on his knees and hung his head toward the floor. I scrunched back on a bright red chaise across from the couch. With my feet straight out, eyes closed and looking toward the ceiling fan, I said, "What is it, Luke? What's going on?"

Luke explained that everything he had said last evening was true with the exception that his pickup hadn't broken down. He had driven by last evening and saw lights so he parked up the road and walked back with the bogus radiator story.

He was sent by a client he couldn't name who was trying to keep tabs on Lenny, who, just recently, was out on parole. Seems like he thought Lenny might lead him to some money that he had forgotten to deliver before he landed in prison.

I didn't know what to say. I guess I shouldn't be surprised because my in my vast experience with men there has always been a vast load of deceit.

Together we went over to Honey's. The door was open just as The Goddess had said, but nothing looked out of place. There was no sign of trouble.

I walked into her bedroom and noted that her bed was made. The towels in the bathroom were dry. It looked to me that Honey had walked into her home and walked out just as fast. Maybe someone was waiting for her.

I checked her closet to see if the gown she wore last evening had been hung up. It hadn't.

"Do we call the authorities, Luke?"

"Let's give this some time Maebeth, Lenny and his friends are not the best negotiators. Cops would just get them to do something dumber than they normally would do."

As we were talking my sister Carmen waltzed in.

Luke did a double take.

"Heard you were down here Maebeth. More trouble with Honey Dean I suppose," Carmen said.

"Carmen, meet Luke Washington." I noted that her left eyebrow has risen about four inches.

Carmen shook Luke's hand.

Carmen has never been a big fan of Honey's. She thinks the drama queen antics are a little more than she wants to deal with at this stage in life. Carmen is my older sister, divorced, and as such still has certain powers over me. Although we look a great deal alike, she is a little taller and a lot more talented. She has the greenest thumb at Heave, loves to cook and sew. We grew up in Lakewood, a suburb of Cleveland. Our dad, Tony, was somewhat of a celebrity during his short life. A sports writer for the *Cleveland Plain Dealer*, he wrote a weekly column called "Caletti's Corner." Mom did the PTA thing, was a crack bridge player and a total crack up.

Carmen and her roommate, Micha Skvarika, along with Julie Baker swim laps every day. At the moment she is wearing a one-piece black tank suit and a bright yellow sarong sashed around her waist.

"I found this," Carmen said handing me a rhinestone earring. "It was by The Way of the Cross and I knew it had to be Honey's. On my way over here to drop it off, I ran into Lily who told me Honey was on the Missing Persons List. I have to give it to that girl. She is never boring."

Luke grabbed the earring and said, "Let's roll."

We all marched out my back door and threaded around the pool to The Way of the Cross. As we approached we heard a faint murmuring. Luke held a hand up indicating for Carmen and me to stay back. He slowly cracked the door but not before drawing a small caliber pistol from the small of his back.

I wondered if he was carrying when we were running this morning, not that anything I had previously thought about him really mattered at this point.

In what seemed like hours but was more like 20 seconds, Luke yelled for us to come in. With Carmen inching up behind me we entered and tiptoed toward the exercise area where Honey was crumbled up on the floor sobbing. Luke was on his knees trying to comfort her and motioning me to come over and help.

Luke explained that he found Honey strapped to a LifeCycle with an old tennis sock stuffed in her mouth. With her makeup viciously smeared she looked like a Peter Max painting. Her front tooth was badly chipped and her fake lashes were half on and half off like little centipedes looking for a place to skitter. She looked exhausted and it probably was because for the last five hours, every time she moved she automatically activated the Lifecycle.

"Thath cockthucker, thath cockthucker," she wailed.

What we deciphered is that after she left my unit, she went to hers and inside were two goons who were FOL. These friends of Lenny wanted to give her a message from the man, which was: Stay the fuck away from anyone asking about him or any of his financial investments. Or, they added, the next cycle she was on would be absent the life part.

Honey figured it had probably taken Lenny about half the time he spent in the slammer to think up something that clever. Lenny is not the sharpest cheese on the cracker.

"Thath lithle prithk," Honey said.

It was the second really intelligent thing she said since the sock was yanked out of her mouth and it made me feel that she's going to be okay.

Carmen took off her yellow sarong and wrapped it around Honey's shoulders. We got her to her feet and half carried her back to her unit. I peeled off her clothes, pulled a big old tee over her, and made her chase an Ambien down with a Diet Coke. In no time she was out.

Something's very wrong here.

Getting to Know You

"**Y**ou got some 'splainin' to do Ricky," I said to Luke as I pointed to the couch in my living room.

Luke kept standing and gently took my hand.

How long has it been since a man had touched me with such tenderness?

For once all the smartass remarks failed me. There was no turning back as he bent down and his lips brushed mine.

I put my arms around him and kissed him back. There was some magical connection with this man and Honey's problems and his vague assignment were not going to get in my way. Maybe it was the gun that was turning me on.

Catching my breath, I whispered, "It's not even noon."

"Best time of the day," Luke said softly while he led me into the bedroom. Slowly we helped each other undress. There was nothing hurried about it. We both seemed to want the moment to last.

This was stagecoach time. You know, you arrive in a small western town on a stagecoach from the east. Your corset is killing you, but you are beyond gorgeous. It's hot as hell, but you're not sweating. Your lovely feathered hat's askew and wisps of golden curls cascade to your delicate shoulders. The horses are panting. Someone opens the stagecoach door. You stand up, look out and faint into the arms of the Marlboro man. From that point on you're not responsible for anything.

Oh hell, have your way with me cowboy.

And when I next looked at the clock on the nightstand, it read 2:46 p.m. I was nestled in the crook of his arm and he was snoring ever so lightly. I quietly grabbed my red silk kimono that was at the foot of the bed and tiptoed out of the bedroom as quietly as Mr. Silverman.

What just happened here?

I glided into my yellow kitchen and plucked a fresh daisy from the centerpiece on the table. Next I toasted some whole wheat bread, scooped on lettuce, tomato and tuna salad, poured a little chablis into two cobalt blue goblets, placed two white linen napkins along with everything else on a tray and headed back to paradise.

Let's hope this wasn't a dream.

Luke stirred as I set the tray on the bench at the bottom of the bed. I sat down next to him and kissed him lightly on the forehead, on each cheek and on his mouth.

"Can this be heaven, Babe?"

"Buttercup, I told you, it's Heave. Sit up darlin' and tell me that after you've tried my cookin'."

Suddenly there was a thump on the bed and there was Mr. Silverman with a look that asked: Did someone say tuna? Luke put his hand out and let the man of the house sniff. Then the purring began as Luke administered a between the ears massage.

"What a ho," I said. "Kinda like his mama."

Luke gave me a tentative look and said, "Maebeth."

"Oh, Luke, I didn't mean anything by that. I never in my life have felt so right about anything."

"Babe, ditto. I'm in your beautiful bed, got a cat purring beside me and we're both looking forward to some tuna," Luke laughed.

"Sugar, that's the first time I've heard you laugh and I could get use to it. No wait, you did laugh at the accommodations in Monistat 1."

"Speaking of which, I guess we should address the future," Luke said with his eyes diverted to the plate I placed on his lap.

"Are you breaking the spell? Do you mean we are going to have wear clothes again, pay our bills, do laundry and all that other stuff?"

With his mouth full of tuna and toast, he gave a dainty dab with the napkin and choked out, "Let's eat first. Have some wine, woman."

The Barbecue

It was dusk when I sauntered out on to my front patio. Lily was on her lawn chair fanning herself with an old *People* magazine.

"Is it true what they say about black boys?" she said.

"Damn it. Are there no secrets? How did you know?"

"Honey, you ain't walkin', you glidin'. Close your front door. Slinky's ex is in town and he's out back barbecuing."

Slinky Rue lives next to Charo. Like Lily, she is tall and very thin. A Eurasian, she was born in Singapore and lived most of her life in Upper Manhattan working as a dancer and translating obscure Japanese texts into English. She and I met in Rome at a time when we were both just out of college and too young to be traveling solo but too old to think it mattered.

Slinky has an uncanny way with both animals and people. She would sit out on her front patio reading and in a short time made friends with a mourning dove that she christened Ms. Early. This bird now marches into her unit, sits on her shoulder and demands attention.

Slinky has been married off and on for more than 35 years to Jack Renkforth, who is quite successful in the import/export business. Basically he imports crappy statues and china and exports most of what he makes to Slinky who is the love of his life. They just have trouble living together and after two divorces and remarriages they still are the best of friends, although I can't remember if they are now married or divorced. Jack, like Luke, is African American, had grown up in the projects and never forgot his origins or his good fortune at never having to return.

I could smell the barbecue.

"Luke said he'd see you out back," Lily said.

"Jesus, it's going to be like the Mills Brothers out there."

"There were four of them, we only got two bros."

As we walked past Carmen and Micha's there was a loud clearing of a throat. This could only be one person. And, that one person had to already know that lo and behold, I had gotten laid. News travels like lightning here.

"Hi Lily. Hi there Maebeth. Anything new?" Carmen asked.

"Yo, big sister, might you be attending Ms. Rue's barbecue this fine evening?"

"My yes, Micha's feeding the darn cats and we'll be along. Save me a seat next to you sis. We need to chat."

"I'd rather drink Clorox," I whispered to Lily.

Lily led the way.

The Roommates
Carmen Carlotta

Look, I'm no Martha Stewart, but it has been said that Carmen Carlotta does a lot of things well.

Don't get me wrong. I've raised a daughter and worked outside the home most of my adult life. It's just that I love being in the kitchen, in the garden, being at the sewing machine.

Now I'm newly retired from the corporate grind and am free to have at all the projects I can dream up.

After being married to a macho Italian loser for a few years, I was almost excommunicated from my parents when I told them I told Guido to hit the road. I raised my daughter, Christine, on my own—no paternal visits or child support.

My sister Maebeth is the reason I'm here at Heave. She had this wild idea of converting this old run-down motel into a shangri la. I thought she was bonkers until I left Cleveland and came out to the desert for a visit.

I was sold and since I moved here I've been able to make it even lovelier. I spend a lot of time with Micha swimming—motion is lotion—so I wanted to make the pool area a showpiece, and it is.

I'd like to think Christine would want to live here someday. Of course, not in this unit with me. Girls need their space.

Karen Oppenheim
Micha Skvarika

Here she goes with the cramped space bit. Yes, even a double unit is crowded for two women, but remember, she's the one who invited me out here. Carmen and I have been friends since grade school, but I don't think either of us realized how such tight quarters would test our friendship. Why in Slovakia, where I'm from, these digs would be considered not exactly castles, but spacious enough and charming.

She thinks I'm high strung. Once heard her tell Maebeth that I make a Nazi look laid back. That's just cruel. I think it's our living situation that makes her tense. One thing we do agree on is unconditional love for my two cats, Salt and Pepper.

And we both have daughters we adore. My girl, Esther, loves to visit, but she has to stay in Monistat 1.

I tell myself that nothing lasts forever so who knows how long we'll be living together.

Good Times

When we got to Slinky's we could hear the laughter coming from the pool area. We walked through her living room to her kitchen and out the back door.

Slinky was holding court in a bright yellow linen dress, her raven hair pulled tightly back into a bun. Jack was standing next to her, one arm around her shoulder, the other holding a margarita. In this little huddle stood Luke, holding a bottle of Sam Adams as well as a look that never left me.

I joined the group.

After welcoming Jack to Heave, I turned to Luke and said, "What have you been up to big boy?"

"Babe, I thought you'd be a little more relaxed this evening."

I grinned.

"Maybe it's kinda like Chinese food and wore off already."

Luke smiled. "God help me, what I have gotten myself into," he said.

We broke away and beelined to the bar where Julie Baker was snuggled up next to a cigar-smoking Moe Feldman, who owns a men's clothing store in Palm Springs. Julie is a workout freak with an eternal tan. She loves men and her little Tibetan terrier, Sue. Moe's mouth was hanging open just enough so as not drop his cigar, as if mesmerized by this 71-year-old who fashioned herself as somewhat of a lounge singer and was singing Nat's part, off-key, to Natalie Cole's "Unforgettable."

Meanwhile, I'm thinking how this all must look to Luke who just got laid a few hours ago and now was watching a bunch of old sirens do their thing.

Charo outdid herself with hors d'ouevres. She had prepared tiny BLT's and everyone was grabbing them as fast as she put them out. The picnic table was covered with a large Mexican serape and bowls of tortilla chips and hot salsa were also getting a lot of attention.

The Goddess marched in, still in her work clothes, with her handbag on one arm and a very cute young man on the other, who was introduced as "Chris, just in from LA."

She and her fetus said they would return after she changed into something more comfortable.

Carmen and Micha arrived. Best friends since grade school, they tolerated each other's craziness. Micha was matter-of-fact about everything and I always thought she would have made a superb executioner in her Slovakian sort of way. There would be no indecision or second thoughts as she put a bead on some poor S.O.B.'s forehead.

By this time Luke had met the entire cast of Heave and most of their animals, both four- and two-legged.

Speaking of which, Beau and Sue were at their best, nudging every leg in sight for a handout. Mr. Silverman was nowhere in sight, but I had the feeling he wasn't far.

Micha's cats, Salt and Pepper, stayed indoors, which was just fine with Slinky's Ms. Early.

Luke and I commandeered two chaises in the corner, stretched out and gazed at the starry desert sky. Neither of us said a word for what seemed like a long time.

Silence never bothers me. In fact, I often prefer it. Over the years, this trait has served me well.

Finally Luke broke the silence. I could tell he was struggling.

"It's hard to put into words what I'm feeling Maebeth. It's been such a long time. In fact, maybe I've never felt this way in my entire life. What I'm trying to say is that we hardly know each other or anything about each other, yet somehow I feel I have known you forever and that there's a sense of destiny to all this. Babe, that's about the longest speech I've ever made. I'm trying to say that you touch me in ways I didn't know possible. You're fun, smart, and you are the most beautiful woman I have ever seen."

I was about to ask him if he could repeat that last part, but my usual wiseass retorts failed me. I was speechless and reached over and took his hand.

"Let's get to know each other Luke. And let's figure out how we can keep you here and get Honey's situation rectified at the same time. Maybe we can make you a little more comfortable in Monistat 1 and you can help us out around here with some of the heavy work we've put off forever. At the same time you could keep an eye on Honey and any unwelcome visitors."

"Don't you have to check that out with your fellow residents?"

"Buttercup, there isn't a single one of them that wouldn't jump your bones in a heartbeat, but yes, I will talk it over with each of them. Meanwhile, you settle into Monistat 1 with extracurricular privileges two units down."

"I think I know where that is," Luke said taking a long pull on his beer.

Everyone was edging over to the barbecue grabbing plastic plates as Charo happily served up chicken and corn. The Goddess, having changed into a long, sleeveless, gauzy white dress was back with her young buck, both looking extremely more relaxed than when they first arrived. Carmen was picking up empty bottles and glasses around the pool. Julie and Moe had disappeared, although Sue was still happily making the rounds. Micha was in a heated argument with Jack about sweat shops, while Slinky checked to see if anyone wanted another drink. Lily had left early complaining of a headache and I made a mental note to check on her later. The only no-shows were Honey and Mr. Silverman.

Luke said if he was going to be the Heave caretaker, he might as well start now. I knew he wanted to check on Honey and look to see if anything was amiss. It already felt so right to have him around.

The Morning After

We all met the next morning over coffee by the pool. It was early so The Goddess could attend before work. Luke had headed into town in search of a hardware store. Everyone looked hung over except Carmen and Micha. It was agreed that Luke was a godsend and could stay as long as he wished. The place needed work and we were all worried about Honey, who still bruised, did manage to put both hands around a cup of coffee and gingerly sip, wincing each time.

Everyone was to come up with a list of things that needed fixed or freshened in their unit. To make it look official, we would provide Luke with a small salary from our reserves in addition to free room and board.

There were a few good-natured snickers when the free room came up.

"Is nookie included in workman's comp?" Julie said.

"Ladies, I just did the math and four out of nine of us got laid yesterday, as far as I know," I said, "so this place isn't exactly a convent."

"You sure as hell don't know everything that goes on around here," Charo said. This caused a few of us to give her the eyeball and wonder about the retired insurance agent who had been stopping by Charo's on a pretty regular basis. Maybe there was more than meatloaf cooking over there.

The Goddess excused herself and Honey said she would walk back with her.

Honey said she was "pithed off" about her tooth and would be seeing her dentist that morning. Carmen had some landscape issues to discuss and wondered whether that was going to be in Luke's domain or remain her job.

We all assured her that no one could ever match the magic she made with her green thumb.

At this point Carmen said, "Oh well, great" and untied her sarong and dived into the deep end of the pool.

I noticed that everyone had gotten quiet before I saw him walking toward the pool. It was The Goddess' Chris wearing a black leather-looking Speedo and a matching bra. Slinky started to cough uncontrollably and I could see her eyes tearing trying to suppress the laughter.

Carmen stopped cold in the middle of a lap, stared, and said, "Jesus, is that twisted or what?"

As if on cue, Moe chomping on a cigar with a beach towel slung over his shoulder and the *Wall Street Journal* under his arm walked out of Julie's back door. Moe was no beauty and needed to back away from the buffet more as his stomach was beyond sucking in. Sue scampered after him, like her mother, loving that a man was in residence.

"What the fuck?" Moe said, checking out Chris.

"Oh, pleeeeeeease," Chris said, "what is all the fuss? I just like dressing up and Moe, if you don't mind my saying so, you could use a little push up in that area yourself."

"It ain't enough to have all these broads around and now they've added a fairy," Moe said.

"You got anything pierced that we don't know about?" Charo asked.

"Look, I'm going for a swim. Come on in Moe, maybe you'll learn something," Chris said.

"Oh, what the hell," Moe said as he dropped his paper and towel on a chair and headed toward the shallow end.

Carmen swam over to Chris to get a better look at the fabric. She was also quite talented with a needle and could whip a bra up for Moe if it came to that.

I started to get up and head back home when I saw Luke come out of the back of Monistat 1 and head toward us. He looked at Chris, Moe and Carmen in the pool and just the slightest hint of a smile was there for a second.

"Good morning, everyone. Aren't we all looking pretty today. Maebeth, you got some chores lined up for me or should I just be a self-starter and put a fresh coat of paint on The Way of the Cross' exterior? That way I can kind of keep an eye on everything out here should things get out of hand."

"Sounds good. You'll find getting an early start before the heat starts baking everything is the way to go around here," I said.

"Well, that's enough for me," Carmen set stepping out of the pool and grabbing her sarong. "Think I'll do a little gardening this morning."

"I'm working this morning on a writing job so I'm heading home. You coming too, Lily?"

Lily unwound her tall frame from the chaise and we walked over to our back doors.

"I think we be needin' a little chat with The Goddess. She might be as interesting as she looks. Got to get to know her better," Lily said.

The Mystery Box

"Holy shit, Maebeth, open the damn door," Carmen yelled.

"What is it Carmen, take it easy?"

"You will never believe what I just found," Carmen said, clutching a metal box about the size of a tool kit. In fact, it was a tool kit.

I opened the door and followed Carmen who rushed over to the kitchen table. She flipped the latch and there in the bottom of the box were stacks of what looked like $100 bills.

"Holy shit is right, where did you find this?"

"I was doing a little planting in the back and noticed one of my cacti tilting sideways near Honey's back door. When I started digging around to replant it, my hoe hit metal. How much do you think is in here?"

"More importantly, what's it doing in our yard?"

This had to involve Honey. I told Carmen to sit tight and went looking for Luke.

I found him, paint brush in hand, and asked him to follow me back to my place.

We didn't say anything to each other and when we entered my unit he immediately went to Carmen who was sitting at the kitchen table with the tool box full of money in front of her.

Luke glared at the box.

Carmen went back over the story for Luke.

"Why must be about half a million in here," Luke said scratching his head. "Does anyone want to make a bet that Honey's not telling us everything?"

Carmen nodded.

Luke pulled up a chair next to Carmen. "Where might Honey be?"

I raised my hand.

"I think she's back from the dentist and taking a nap. She's worn out."

"Well, let's wake the little songbird up and see what's going on. This looks like it was planted in the backyard recently and quickly," Luke said.

The three of us walked over to Honey's front door and I knocked. We could hear some movement and finally the door opened with a squinting Honey rubbing her eyes and dressed in a long, dingy white t-shirt.

"What's up?" she asked.

"How about lots of bucks buried in your backyard," Luke said.

Honey reacted with a theatrical look of surprise. And then in a stage whisper she said, "You're kidding."

"Honey, this doesn't look good. You have some very bad boys looking for this and they damn near killed you trying to find out about it. Now you owe it to all of us at Heave to fess up. This ain't the inner city," I said with my hands on my hips while giving her a hard look.

"Oh, Christ," Honey sobbed. "It was sent here in a Fed Ex box last week. I know Lenny's involved with this. I tried calling the name and company of the sender but there is no such person or firm. I didn't know what to do so I hid it. And when I got roughed up I thought if I told them that is all they'd need and they'd kill me."

"Any ideas, Sherlock?" I asked Luke.

"Let's all go back to your place Maebeth and try to figure this out," Luke said.

The four of us trounced back to my place. My door was unlocked and there on the kitchen table was the half million.

"You white folk are a little casual when it comes to the criminal mind," Luke said. "Anyone could have strolled in here and helped himself."

"Oh yeah, Charo probably needed some egg money. And Julie might have been short for her manicure. And of course Micha was probably low on kielbasa. For God's sake, Luke," I said.

"Money does crazy things to people. How well do any of you know that two-piece wonder that's holed up with The Goddess?" Luke said.

"You made your point," I said.

Just then the door opened and it was Slinky.

"Hey, I'm going into Palm Springs. Anybody want to tag along? Do a little shopping, have some lunch and maybe grab a movie?"

Her eyes moved over to the kitchen table and she let out a shriek.

"My, my, we could do some very serious shopping. Maebeth, have you been holding back on us. Say, just what do those copywriting jobs pay these days? Damn, I have to run down and grab Julie. She dreams of having this much to spend."

"Why don't we just put an ad in *The Desert Sun*?" Luke said. "Something like: 'Dumb Clucks Find Big Bucks at Heave.' Of course we'd want to include our address and phone number so that if by chance the crooks can read, we've made it a little easier for them. No, better yet we publish a map on how to get to Heave. It could be drawn like one of those old treasure maps."

"Knock it off," I said. "Man, when you get on a roll, there's no stopping you."

In walked Julie and her dog, Sue.

"Yikes, this is good," she said. "Wait till I tell Moe. Sue, get over here and take a look at all this loot."

Luke got up and went over to the couch and plopped down. He put his cap over his face and was deathly quiet. It was enough to shut us all up. We had a problem.

The Fashionista
Julie Baker

So I like clothes, men and looking hot. Who doesn't? Well, there are some, but certainly none of my friends at Heave. At 71 years, do I really care?

I wasn't always this way. As I kid I was overweight, but during my sophomore year I finally got my period, the weight dropped off and I was, or so they say, a stunner.

Did a little modeling—furs, cocktail dresses, that kind of thing. I'm the gal who would interrupt your lunch to show off my wares and tell you where you could buy them. That lasted a few years and then I got serious and decided to become a stewardess. They tell me now that that's not politically correct and it should be flight attendant. Oh, hooey, honey! Only managed one flight and knew I wasn't the waitress type.

Being a Texan, I still say things that aren't meant to be mean. Like coloreds is how I refer to, well, coloreds.

Men have always been attracted to me. Before I met Ronald, I had six engagement offers. I still think about those boys and wonder where they are today, but Ronald was a mature man and the love of my life. We had two kids, Austin and Daisy. Both good kids and both have done well. When Ronald was killed in a car accident, I thought my life was over, but it's funny how time heals.

Today I'm happily single and seeing Moe Feldman. He's good to me, but I could do without the cigars. He takes me to nice places, is a sharp dresser and has a big personality. Plus, he loves to dance.

Did I mention I also sing? Think Michelle Pfeiffer in The Fabulous Baker Boys. That kinda didn't work out, but it was fun trying.

Today my days are spent sunning by the pool, playing bridge and best of all, cuddling with my Tibetan terrier, Sue. She's one of the best things that ever happened to me.

The Plan

The plan was pretty simple. After swearing the tribe at Heave to keep quiet about the motherlode, Luke and I jumped into his pickup and headed to Palm Springs where I had a safe deposit box at First National Bank.

As we were heading down Palm Canyon Drive we passed by the Plaza Theater, home of the Palm Springs Follies, which was a vaudeville-type show featuring long-legged lovelies age 50 and up.

"Might you be interested in a little tourist fun?" I asked.

"Got enough old broads where I work," Luke grumbled, showing a side I hadn't seen before.

"Excuse me, Mr. Washington, our situation is bad but it isn't a goddamn tsunami."

"Look Babe, we're dealing with some boys who play for keeps. This isn't our money and I'm working for someone who flunked charm school and is not going to be happy when he finds out we found the money and are holding on to it."

Man, he's a stone fox even when he's pissed.

"Things got complicated when Honey got beat up. I think we need to sit tight and see what Lenny's next move is because we know he's not going away," Luke said.

I went into the bank with my shopping bag full of cash. When I came out I saw that Luke was standing outside the truck talking on a cell phone. He saw me and mumbled his goodbye to whoever was on the other end of the call.

51

"Got an old friend who's always wanted to visit the desert," Luke said. "Thought this might be a good time to beef up the bunker so he's heading out here from LA and will have the great good fortune to experience Monistat 1 for a few days. His name is Frank Sellars."

As we were driving back to Heave, Luke filled me in on Frank's background. The two had done some undercover work together years ago. Frank was divorced and retired which gave him plenty of time to be quietly bored. He had been on the job for more than 20 years...the last quarter as a homicide detective. Although he had hated the bureaucracy of the department, the work was his life and now with too much time on his hands, he was aching to be of use to someone.

It was about noon so we pulled into Manhattan Bagel for lunch. As we settled into a booth, Luke's cell phone rang and he glanced at the number and excused himself.

I ordered us each a Diet Coke and wondered again how much I really knew this man who already had lodged a permanent place in my heart.

When he returned we studied the menu and each ordered a Cobb salad after which there was an uneasy silence.

"Okay Luke, none of us at this point has a lot of days above ground. I know you have a number of lifetimes that we haven't shared and I, too, have a shitload full of baggage, but that comes with the territory at this age. I just need to feel a little more secure that you are who you say you are."

"Oh, Babe," he said, reaching over and dabbing his napkin at the corner of my mouth, "bleu cheese looks so damn sexy on you."

Hello, Frank

Early the next morning I slipped on a pair of gray jersey drawstring shorts and a pink cotton tank with *How about never?* scrolled daintily across the chest in rhinestones, laced up my running shoes and hit the road. I hadn't run but a half a mile when I saw a dirty, black, old model Ford gunning down the road in my direction. As it sped past me creating a cloud of dust, I could see it was heading toward Heave.

Must be Sellars, I thought, and continued my run.

When I got back to Heave, the car was parked in front of Monistat 1. After I showered and changed clothes, I went over to see what was up. No one was at M-1 and I could smell breakfast coming from Charo's.

Luke, and whom I suspected was Sellars, were polishing off a plate of eggs, bacon and hash browns with Charo scurrying around like a new bride.

"Oh, here's the queen of Heave," said Luke.

"That supposed to be a compliment?" I inquired.

"Maebeth, meet Frank Sellars, LAPD retired."

Sellars looked like he'd been caught in a blender. Although his hair was dishwater blond, it was going gray at the temples and his gut belied a Gold's membership. He had on a black, threadbare golf shirt that hung out over a pair of loose-fitting jeans and scratched-up cowboy boots that had seen better days. A black LAPD ball cap was hanging on the back of the dinette chair.

"How do you do, Maebeth," Sellars said as he stood with his mouth still

53

massaging a strip of bacon while he wiped his hand on a crumpled paper napkin.

"Glad to have some reinforcements. I don't know how long Luke is going to hold up," I said trying to stifle a grin.

Luke's eyes narrowed.

"Oh, I think I'll find the strength somewhere. I've been filling Frank in on our situation and we've come up with a plan of sorts. We are going to leak the word that we've found a cache and have headed back to LA with it. Honey is not to know the truth, which is that we're not moving the money anywhere, but whoever is so interested can come ask us where it is. We can try to flush them out."

Do I like this idea? That means he leaves.

Just as Luke was finishing, Micha bounded into the room wanting to know if Charo had an extra can of tuna for Salt and Pepper. She screeched to a halt like a Jet Blue with a landing gear malfunction.

After introductions, it was clear she might be the fifth Heave resident to get lucky this week. Frank and she made an instant connection. She mentioned she had just made kielbasa and invited everyone over for dinner that evening. I secretly enjoyed the fact that my sister, a stickler on manners, was about to experience dinner with LAPD's finest.

Frank mentioned that it would be a nice way to spend the evening before he sped back to LA early the next morning, but that he would be coming back in a few days. Micha quickly interjected that she had been thinking of going into LA to do some shopping and could she catch a ride. She had a friend she could stay with.

"Would love the company," Frank said.

I excused myself citing unfinished work to do and extended my regrets that I would be unable to attend the evening's Polka Festival or whatever.

Luke said that he would stay on at Heave while Frank and Micha drove to LA. He wanted to be around in case any thugs showed up.

Amen, and thank you Jesus.

The Goddess checked in to say "good morning" and was looking more gorgeous than ever in a long black skirt and a white silk blouse with a few more buttons open than usual. Chris was evidently not as light in the loafers as Moe had thought.

On the Road Again

They took off early the next morning. "Mickie" as Frank called his new friend rode shotgun with a picnic basket tucked between them and a serious looking cardboard box wrapped tightly with burlap string on the back seat. This I was told later was for the benefit of anyone interested in documenting their departure.

Carmen, delighted with her newfound space, planned to go in to Palm Springs with Julie and have lunch with Moe who had gotten interested in Chris' two-piecer and was going to have Carmen work up some prototypes.

Luke had gone back to Monistat 1 to make a few phone calls and get the word out that the money had been found. He was also going to stall his client, telling him that he had a new lead and things looked positive.

Slinky was packing to go back to Manhattan for a few weeks with Jack. Summer in the desert was always a good time to head somewhere else, but I couldn't imagine that steamy New York would be much better. Slinky still had a lot of friends in the Big Apple and went back periodically to get her juices flowing. She needed to travel and once told me that she was happiest going through the Suez Canal on a freighter.

Lily would also be leaving in a few days to visit with her two sons in Savannah.

It seemed that everyone was from somewhere else, but what brought them together felt more than coincidence. Heave had become home for all of us and there was a solid sense of family that gave each of us a modicum of peace that hadn't been there in the earlier parts of our lives. We all by this time had established solid identities and accepted each other as is. Not that there wasn't a little tension at times, but how could there not be with nine women living in such a small community.

The World Traveler

Slinky Rue

"What's that, Julie? No, I don't want to come out and lay by the pool."
I adore the Heave ladies, but I really like my downtime. Being quiet with my work translating texts takes my full concentration. Not that I'm a loner. Who could be living between Charo and Julie who always have something going.

And being Eurasian, I've already got a nice glow and don't care for those aging sun rays.

Yes, I was born in Singapore and have traveled the world, mostly with Jack Renkforth, my husband, or is he now my ex-husband? Anyway, we've been married, divorced, remarried and I'm not sure where we are now. Bottom line is we can't live with or without each other. Kind of like Liz and Richard.

Most of my younger years were spent in Upper Manhattan where for decades I belonged to an elite group of high-kick dancers. Being over 6' tall, thin and having shiny, raven-colored hair helped me stand out. That's how I got the name Slinky, because I could really move.

Heave has been wonderful for me. You'd think after my travels and life in the big city, the desert would have been a culture shock. Not so. I love the tranquility and serene beauty of this piece of the world. I once said my favorite journey was going through the Suez Canal, but now it's about sitting quietly on my porch whispering to Ms. Early, a mourning dove that has adopted me. We are best friends.

My other bestie is Maebeth, to whom I shall be eternally grateful for telling me about Heave. She is always the first person my sister, Mavis, wants to see when she visits me. There's just something so authentic about dear Maebeth.

News from Honey

Back to reality. I decided that I should buckle down, pay some bills and bill some clients. I'd set up an office area in the corner of my living room.

While waiting for the computer to come to life I went out to the refrigerator and popped open a Diet Coke. Mr. Silverman ambled out from under the kitchen table and gave me the second best "good morning" a girl could get. He rubbed his big gray body hard against my leg and the purring beat the hell out of anything Mozart could have composed. I scooped up my big boy and assured him he was the best cat in the universe and that I had known a lot of cats.

With Mr. Silverman snuggled happily in my lap I decided to check my emails. There were 23 of which most were spam urging me to purchase a walk-in bath tub, to check out the Neptune Society and to buy some Viagra.

I saw that there was one from Honey. I opened it and froze.

maebitch we got honey and we keepin the ho til we git whats mine. meat me in the parkin lot at cirkle k in thermal with the mony and a lone or else. Tomorow 10:30 in the mornin yur frind lenny

I quickly dialed Luke's cell, got him on the first ring and told him to get over here. He was at my computer a few minutes later and already on the phone to Frank telling him to turn around and come back.

Late that evening we devised a plan. Luke and Frank would stake out the Circle K early the next morning. I was to arrive promptly at 10:30 a.m. with the bogus box of money on the front seat and to remain in the car.

Neither Frank nor Luke felt that Lenny had the brainpower to pull this off, but no one doubted that he was nuts and a loose cannon. Everyone was worried about Honey, but thankfully we were going to keep our plans secret and with so many Heave residents planning an exodus, we didn't want to worry anyone. We also felt that the danger quotient had risen enough to warrant as few people around as possible for their own safety.

Frank and Micha decided to stretch their legs before retiring. Luke was going to bunk in with me, giving Frank his digs at Monistat 1.

I said good night to Frank and his new friend, verified we'd meet at my place at 7:00 a.m., closed the door and headed to the kitchen for some Sleepytime Tea.

Luke followed and observed, "Yep, I'd imagine you'd need that what with a night with me ahead of you."

"I just need to calm down. When I think of poor Honey, I could cry. That Lenny is an animal. How could she have married that jerk in the first place?"

Luke pulled me toward him and placed my head against his chest. "Take it easy, Babe. We have to have our wits together for tomorrow."

He headed to the bathroom for a shower.

"Make that a cold shower, hot stuff," I yelled after him.

"There's room in here for you, Babe," he yelled.

Oh what the hell. Being filthy and miserable isn't going to bring Honey back.

Fifteen minutes later we cuddled up in bed and I had found something better than Sleepytime Tea to take the edge off.

At 10:10 the next morning I was in my Honda Accord headed for the Circle K. Luke and Frank had left hours earlier. Both of my legs were shaking and it was hard to keep the car steady on the road. I pulled into an empty space and noted there were three cars parked in the lot and no one appeared to be in them. It was 10:25 and I had no clue as to where Luke and Frank would be hiding.

A skinny man in a white t-shirt, John Deere cap and tight jeans came out the front door carrying a big coffee. He got into a blue Ford pickup, took a gulp of coffee and backed out.

Another guy with a fat gut came out the front door carrying a bag of food in one hand and a gigantic cup of something in the other. He sat the cup on the hood and ripped open a package of Twinkies before he got into his car.

Just then a white SUV pulled into the lot. Its windows were deeply tinted and I couldn't see who was driving. I had never met Lenny in person so I wasn't sure what he looked like. However, I had seen his mug shot so had some idea of his overall appearance.

Next what looked like a Sumo wrestler poured out of the passenger side. He was not only big and baldheaded but mean looking.

I stayed put.

The driver's side of the car opened and a real greaser I assumed was Lenny got out. Behind him, jumping out of the SUV was Honey wearing a big smile and looking damn good for a hostage.

The two of them came over to my car and Lenny scoped out the passenger seat, saw the package and said, "That'd be my money?"

"Honey, GET IN THE CAR," I screamed.

Honey let out a wail and sobbed, "I'm staying with Lenny. I love him. I'm sorry Maebeth, I can't help it. I just love him."

If I'd have had a gun in my hand, I would have shot them both.

Out of nowhere Luke and Frank appeared with Frank surprising the Sumo bodyguard who was quickly subdued by the site of Frank's pistol.

Luke approached Lenny with a menacing look, his hand partway in the pocket of his windbreaker.

"The broad's goin' with me," Lenny said.

"That right, Honey?" Luke asked.

"Oh, I'm so sorry to have caused all this fuss, but after last night, I can see what I saw in Lenny all along.

He's just had some bad breaks and I want to give us another chance. Of course he still wants that darn money."

Luke reached in my car and grabbed the bogus package, shoved it into Lenny's arms and said, "Okay wiseass, each of us is getting nada but take this as a reminder that you're screwing around with the wrong people and if I ever see your sorry ass again, I will personally put you out of commission for the rest of your life and that might not be for too long the way you're going. Take one step forward or hurt that woman you've conned again into going with you, and I will have the police on your ass so fast you won't know what hit you. Walk away now and keep walking you little prick and you may have bought yourself some time before your next fuck up. By the way, have you checked in with your parole officer or would you like me to save you the call?"

Lenny appeared to have gotten the message. If for nothing else, Luke was a good bit taller with a body that had seen a lot of workouts—and not just with me. Honey was bed-sheet white. Lenny grabbed her arm and they got back in the SUV with Sumo boy right behind them. They tore out of the lot and Luke, Frank and I just looked at each other.

"Do you think this is over?" I asked.

"As far as getting the money back, it's over," Luke said. "I gave instructions yesterday to wire it back to my client. Honey is a grown woman and she's made her choice, at least until he smacks her around the next time."

"Let's get some breakfast," Frank said.

"I'm going to pass. This is a little too much excitement for me," I said.

"Take the car, Frank," Luke said. "I'll go back with Maebeth and catch up with you later at Heave."

Goodbyes

We were sitting on my couch sipping Diet Cokes.

"Will you be going back now, Luke?"

"Yes. I've got a lot of work to catch up on. Let's take this time to think us through, Babe. You have changed my life and I don't want to ever lose you. I'd like you to come to Los Angeles soon and spend some time in my world. I feel such a part of this family you've created here at Heave. Let's see what our next step is."

Should I break down and cry now or should I try to be the strong woman he thinks I am. Damn. This is why I never ever want to get involved with a man again. My life was going fine. A little boring, but secure in my world and now here we goddamn go again.

"Are you leaving today?"

"Yes, he said, brushing my hand against his lips. I'll get my things together and be out of here before noon. I'll call you when I get home."

He pulled me up off the couch and we held each other like this might be the last time. My emotions were clanging around so much that I was dizzy. First the madness of the morning and now my heart felt like someone was scraping it with a sharp knife.

We walked outside and saw Micha getting into Frank's car. Carmen was handing her the replenished picnic basket and she was waving goodbye, happy as I've ever seen her. The two of them both seemed so uncomplicated.

I hugged Frank and wished Micha a good time. She was wearing extremely short denim shorts and a navy boatneck top. They were definitely going to have a good time.

Luke continued down to Monistat 1.

Carmen came over and put her arm around my shoulders. That did it. I burst into tears and buried my face into her Jessica McClintock-scented neck. She stroked my hair with her other arm and directed me back into her unit. Salt and Pepper were perched on her couch and she shooed them off and we sat down.

"Oh, sweetie," Carmen said, "I know you thought a lot of Luke but try to look at it with clearer eyes if you can. Luke has a whole other life you know nothing about. You went into this so fast. You hardly know him. Plus, he's black and you're white and that's a whole different enchilada."

"We're not white, we're Italian," I said.

Carmen laughed.

"We are so different and I don't think I've ever loved you more. No one knows you like I do, Maebeth. You're not the tough nut everyone thinks you are.

"Now, let's think about lunch. I have some leftover London broil from last night. What say I make us some sandwiches with horseradish, dill pickles and my fresh peach cobbler." She was already on the way to the kitchen.

Christ, this is Charo in training.

"Actually sis, what would be good right now is a bottle of Jack Daniel's and a 45 to blow my brains out. To go, if you don't mind. Wouldn't want all that blood and vomit all over your Martha Stewart digs."

"Sit your butt down, here's a copy of *Vanity Fair*, and for God's sake button it up while I make lunch."

Just then I heard a car door slam and went to the window to see Luke pulling out of the Heave parking lot and heading west to LA.

Your loss, buster.

Two Best Friends

I wasn't home but 15 minutes when Julie called asking if I'd like to have Sue for a sleepover. Julie was going to spend the night at Moe's and then head out early the next morning for LA. They were taking Carmen's prototypes of the leather-like two-piece into a manufacturer for a meeting.

"Julie, bring that little Tibetan over here this minute. She's just what I need," and I proceeded to tell her what had happened with Honey and with Luke's departure.

I had no more put the receiver down when the phone rang again. It was Honey and I could barely hear her over her whispery, whimpering voice.

"Oh gawd, can you ever forgive me? I guess I just hadn't had good sex for such a long time. I don't know. Maybe I should always do it with my hands bound with rope and a gag."

Maybe Lenny wasn't as dumb as I thought. Especially about that gag part.

Honey assured me that she was okay, but that Lenny was pissed as hell about the money. Yet no money vs. going back to the slammer was a no-brainer even for Lenny.

There was a knock on the door and Sue bounded in ahead of Julie who had packed a TOD bag with Sue's blanket, pills, treats, and stuffed dolphin. Sue jumped up on the couch and started to ram me with her head. Looks like Mr. Silverman was going to have some competition this evening.

I handed the phone to Julie, "It's Honey, the honeymooner. Ask her if she's going to keep her unit or move. Remind her that there's a waiting list a lot longer that dickweed Lenny's johnson."

While they chatted I got up and put a bowl of ice water down on the floor for Sue.

Julie was off the phone and informed me that Honey said she would never give up her home at Heave. She said she got comfort knowing she had place she could go and added something about all our unconditional love.

I didn't want to touch that unconditional love thing because I was having some dark thoughts, yet she was right.

Heave would always be there for all of us through all the starts and stops in life. Heave was our home, our safety net and a hell of a long way from assisted living.

Julie left to go to Palm Springs. It was dusk. I opened a beer, grabbed another and Sue and headed down to Charo's.

Charo was sitting on her glider out on her front porch watching the sun go down. She looked tired. I handed her a beer. She smiled, patted the seat next to her and said, "It must be about Luke. Come here pumpkin, and tell me all about it."

I thought I had cried every last tear I had, but it erupted again as I slumped down next to Charo and poured it all out. Sue looked upset, so I stopped the self-pity and scooped her up where she promptly jumped on to Charo's lap. Charo, Heave's wisest woman, had lived longer than any of us, seen more, and kept going forward at a pace that dazzled all of us. We could hardly keep up and no one matched her generosity, warmth and ability to live in the now.

Charo held my hand and said, "I thought when my husband died that it was the worst thing that would ever happen to me. I miss him to this day and our time together was so short. Going without a new car, vacations, the latest dress—none of this mattered to me because even as a young girl I knew about the irreplaceables. Well, I was wrong about a lot of things because when I lost my daughter I doubted if I could ever go on. But I did and whatever is to be for you and Luke, you will go on. Maebeth, you're not a quitter. The fact that you created our Heave has already set you so far above so many other women who don't have the creativity or won't make the effort to change things. You are amazing, dear girl, and I'm so glad that you had this time with someone who so touched your soul. It will take a lot more than a man to stifle your spirit."

"Oh Charo, I so love you." I know this isn't cancer and I'm glad I didn't hold back for fear of getting hurt, even though right this moment I feel like someone threw a bowling ball at my stomach."

Charo lifted Sue onto the porch and said, "How about some popcorn and another beer?"

The Godmother
Charo Blake

Although I'm the oldest Heaver, I can wrap rings around some of these other ladies in more areas than they can imagine. I'm keeping some stuff to myself because I don't want to cause anyone to blush.

My daughter, Sarah, was the best young woman you'd ever meet. She was a peach. Why the good Lord took her home so young is still a mystery, but I guess She just wanted to be with her, too.

In addition to being the oldest, I'm also the tiniest Heavette at 5'1". Guess my personality makes up for what got short-changed when it comes to height.

Everyone stops by my designer kitchen to visit and taste my vittles. Honey, whoever said butter, cream and sugar were bad ain't my kind of folk. We're all going to the boneyard, but my folk will be smilin'.

Take this example:

Divinity

3 cups white sugar

2/3 cup white Karo syrup

2/3 cup water

2 egg whites, stiffly beaten

1 tsp vanilla

1 cup chopped walnuts

Combine sugar, syrup and water. Boil to medium stage of 240 degrees. Slowly pour half the mixture over the egg whites. Cook remaining syrup mixture to a hard boil of 280 degrees. Continue beating until the mixture holds its shape when dropped from a spoon. Add vanilla and nuts. Drop by teaspoons on a piece of aluminum foil.

I once said to Maebeth, "Will you remember me when I'm gone?"

Being Maebeth, she chuckled and said, "Charo, my waist will never forget you and neither will my heart."

That made me happy.

A Scare

"You fat fuck."

It's all I could think of saying to myself as I laced up brand new New Balance 8.5 D-width running shoes and headed for the front door. Today's green tee read *Hi! You'll Do* in large white letters. Thank that same God that I had on drawstring shorts because I was getting a gut. Might be that so-called zero-calorie flavored water that I'd be drinking by the gallon. Thought that was supposed to be healthy and hydrating.

It was three weeks since Luke went back to LA. Lots of phone calls and promises in between but neither of us appeared able or maybe wanted to move the relationship forward from its park position.

I was beginning to wonder if my mid-life sexual revolution might not have been such a good idea after all.

I mean a lot of women have good lives being celibate.

Look at Lily, Charo and Carmen. They were complete women. Come to think of it, I wasn't all that sure about Charo's celibacy and Carmen was secretive. And Lily still wasn't back, so who knows what's up with her when she's back in her old stomping grounds.

So out of all nine residents, meet the Virgin Maebeth.

Very possibly, I was the smartest of all. In fact, I had recently read an article saying that more men than women want marriage and a family. No shit, Einstein. I could have used a wife years ago. Cook my food, wash my clothes, clean the house and take her out on Saturday nights. Somehow, the price always seemed too high. Plus TV was at its best on Saturday nights.

About a mile into my run, I heard a car coming up behind me. It was Carmen in her shiny new Acura. I stopped at the side of the road as she slowed.

"Get in, Maebeth. It's Charo, something's wrong."

Oh God, I promise I will never ask for anything else ever but please let Charo be okay.

I jumped in the car and Carmen related how she had just come from Charo's. When she knocked on the door, there was no answer so she went over to Monistat 1 where we had a set of keys for every unit, and unlocked Charo's door.

Poor Charo was on the kitchen floor, dazed but conscious. She said she had felt dizzy and the next thing she knew she woke up on the floor.

Carmen got her on the couch and went to get me. We were out in the boonies and she felt that we could get her to JFK Memorial faster than it would take us to summon 911.

We got a reluctant Charo into the car and into Emergency at the hospital. After leafing through old magazines, a doctor came out to tell us they were going to keep Charo a few days for tests. He said they were taking her to her room and it was probably best if we let her rest and come by tomorrow.

Carmen and I were drained. It was now about 1:30 p.m. and we were hungry so we stopped in Indio at Teresa's, a popular, funky Mexican restaurant, and dove into a few margaritas and enchilada and taco combinaciones.

I thought I probably should run all the way home to work off the lard load but warmed by the tequila and the very thought of the desert heat caused me to reconsider.

Carmen and I decided we would only tell Julie and The Goddess about Charo. Why upset Lily and Slinky when we didn't know what the story was yet. As for Honey, she was on her own as far as I was concerned. And Micha was still in LA planning a permanent move or so it appeared as her romance with Frank was sizzling. Carmen was already asking if you could Fed Ex cats and was thrilled at the prospect of living alone again.

I was still feeling no pain when I got home and bravely decided to call Luke.

He answered on the second ring. Just hearing "hello" set me sobbing.

"Maebeth, Maebeth, are you okay? What's going on?"

Now I was not only fat, but my mascara was streaking down my cheeks as I choked out the story of Charo.

"I'm on my way. Need to tie up a few things here, but I'll be there first thing tomorrow and I'll take you to the hospital."

After a few insincere protests—forgetting that I had morphed into Shamu—I agreed to wait for him in the morning.

He's Baaaack!

At dawn I was laced up and out the door after a short walk with Sue. The desert was beautiful at this time of day. The sun was just starting to wake, casting a pinkish hue on the mountains. The birds had a cacophony of tunes going and I felt renewed as I hit the road and headed toward The Crossings. I had left plenty of time to get back home, shower and spruce up before Luke arrived.

What had it been? Almost a month since we'd seen each other, but we had kept in contact over the phone. Luke wasn't much for emails. Might have had something to do with his NSA mentality and paper trails.

I had gotten to know him better though. He had said he was semi-retired, but I didn't think that was quite the case. And I got the impression that he was a loner and a lot more successful in business than he'd let on. Nothing he was direct about, but more the way he talked when I asked what he was up to.

I was building up a good sweat. Tucked some wayward strands of hair behind my right ear and pulled the neck of my gray sleeveless tee up over my face to absorb some of the moisture. Today's quote printed in bright red letters across my chest read *HELP ME RHONDA*.

Thoughts of Charo had been popping into my head throughout my run. I had called the night nurse before I left Heave and was told that she was resting comfortably, whatever that means. The dead rest comfortably. No place to have to go. No bills to pay.

When The Crossings finally came into view, I slowed it down. I was bending over in front of The Café trying to catch my breath when I heard a car tearing down the road. I heard its brakes screech and felt a cloud of dust raining down upon me.

"Son of a bitch," I shouted as I whirled around and spotted a black Jaguar convertible, top down and a dude with a baseball cap pulled low.

"Nice view, Babe. You almost caused an accident. You think Charo might need a roommate?"

My heart stopped and my knees turned to Jell-O. I was speechless for once in my life. God, this man looked good.

And here I was with too tight drawstring shorts, scuzzy tank top, ruby earrings, frizzy hair and sweat everywhere.

Luke slowly got out of the car and stood by the passenger door with a big grin and his arms outstretched.

I didn't move.

"Babe, there are about three ways this can go. We can do it here in the sand, do it in the car or hop in and I'll take you home and we'll do it there."

My composure was starting to come back.

"Look sport, I'm not that easy. I expect at least breakfast and a movie or something like that."

"I take that as we'll do it at your place and I'll cook breakfast for you after, if you're strong enough to hold a fork and chew."

I ran toward him and jumped into his arms, locking my legs around his waist. Then it was one deep, long, oxygen-starved kiss.

He's kissing me like they do in the movies.

Neither of us could really talk. There were lots of "God, you taste good," "I love the way you smell" and "I can't get enough of you."

With his arm around my shoulders, Luke walked me over to the passenger door, opened it and gently closed the door.

Soon we were flying toward Heave and how I felt I looked didn't seem to matter. If there was a litmus test, I had passed with flying colors. This could be one of the better things about middle age. We get way past the surface because we know authentic when we feel it.

A Great Way to Start the Day

Virgin Maebeth was no more.

Luke was rustling up omelets and I was back in the shower for the second time that morning and it wasn't even 8:00 a.m. Sue was standing right next to him at the stove, hoping for a handout.

I jumped out of the shower, wrapped a towel around me and headed for the kitchen.

He was beyond gorgeous. Eat your heart out Seal.

Barefoot and in pressed denims and a navy polo shirt, he turned toward me and grinned.

"You better be careful, missy. That towel looks like it might be easy to tug off and start something up that will ruin my culinary efforts."

"Hmmm," I said. "Buttercup, not in front of Sue. Did you notice that there might have been a little more to love this time? I've gained eight pounds since I last saw you. I thought about greeting you at the door this morning with a white sheet around me so you'd think I was ready but wouldn't see the damage."

"Babe, don't scare me with that white sheet talk. Are you messin' with me?"

"Oooops, you know what I mean."

"Maebeth, you are perfect. Didn't I just show you how much I love you and missed you?"

Did I just hear the "L" word?

Just then I heard a scratching on the back screen door. It was Mr. Silverman back from a night of being Mr. Silverman. I unlatched the screen door and he strode in giving Luke a could-care-less look, glanced at Sue and headed for the living room.

"I see that feline really missed me," Luke said. "Mr. S. has a lot competition for mama's affection."

"No contest," I replied flippantly. "If it comes down to I have to choose, ciao baby. The cat stays."

An hour later we were walking down the hospital corridor heading toward Charo's room. She was sitting up in bed picking at a tray of food.

"Thank heavens you're here, Luke. You understand the importance of quality nutrition. Get me out of here before I croak from this crap. I think they're trying to kill me."

I was so glad to see that Charo was back to her old self that all I could do was grin. Tears started to spring from the corners of my eyes, but I waved them off and rushed toward her.

"Old woman, you will do anything to get my man back here. Seriously, how are you feeling and what did the doctor have to say?"

"They want to do more tests. I'm in prison and I have to break out of here. I feel fine. Look at all these flowers. That hand-picked job is from Carmen who was here a little while ago. I feel like I'm laid out at Molten's Funeral Home."

"Well, you're here for a little longer. Is there anything I can bring you?" I asked.

"Maybe you and Luke could pick me up tomorrow and we could stop somewhere and get some real food," Charo said. "Of course, by tomorrow I could be dead from starvation."

"You have a deal, girlfriend," I said.

"Oh, look," Charo said, "here's Lester bearing gifts."

Lester, the mysterious insurance agent we'd heard a little about, was carrying a large bouquet and a big teddy bear with a big pink ribbon around its neck that read "Be my honey bear."

Charo did the introductions and we all shook hands.

Luke cleared his throat, put his hand on my elbow and said we were going to be leaving and would find out when we could pick her up tomorrow.

Each of us gave her a peck on the forehead and headed toward the corridor.

At the nurse's desk I asked if Charo's doctor was in the vicinity. Just then a tall, white-coated, gray-haired man strode purposely toward us.

Dr. Metzbaum explained that although more tests were scheduled today, he felt that Charo was overdoing it and had been dehydrated which caused the dizziness and subsequent fall. He said she needed to realize that her body was old and she couldn't do all the things she was doing 25 years ago and still thought she could do.

Hi, Sam

The phone was ringing when we got back to Heave. It was Sam, Charo's grandson, who had been trying to call Charo but getting no answer. Sam was a successful interior designer who had built a terrific career in New York. He said he had some business in LA and had planned to visit his grandmother but after hearing the news would extend his visit.

I told him that would be a great tonic for her and he could stay at Monistat 1, which I explained to him was our Presidential Suite. Although Sam's mother, Sarah, had lived here, he had been busy getting established in the Big Apple and when he would be out west he would have a car pick up his mom and grandmother and spirit them to LA for a weekend.

Like Charo and Sarah, Sam was an excellent cook and promised to prepare a feast for everyone when he arrived.

This promised to be fun.

Luke was at my front door during the call hearing just snatches of the conversation. He was talking to someone, but I couldn't make out whom.

As I headed for the front door, I could hear Lily. I rushed out and put my arms around her and told her how glad I was to see her.

Luke had updated her on Charo.

We asked her to come in for a beer, but she said she was still unpacking and would catch us later and fill us in on her trip. Beau was already inside on her bed, sacked out after the long ride.

Luke and I plopped down on the sofa with two Sam Adams Lights and Sue.

"So Charo's Sam is an interior decorator and a good cook. Does he like the ladies?" Luke asked.

"Why Luke Washington, might that be a little stereotyping I'm detecting? I am surprised."

"Just wondering. I could care less."

"Good, now let's see what I have for lunch. I imagine some black-eyed peas, grits and greens would sound real good about now."

I had almost made it off the couch when Luke grabbed me from behind and lifted me off the ground.

"Woman, get into the kitchen and whip up some grub. And when you're done, call whoever is around here at this god-forsaken place and tell them I'm barbecuing tonight and they're all invited. I'm going to run out to the store and get some food."

"Got it, chief. Could you maybe put me down before I bust a gut laughing at all this he-man stuff and you hurt your back?"

"Oh, and that reminds me," Luke said. "Maybe Julie could call Moe and invite him over. I've run out of household hints and beauty tips and could use a tad of testosterone."

Wow, this feels like we're a couple.

Some quick calls and Carmen, Lily, The Goddess and Chris, Julie and Moe, who were on their way back from LA, were "all in" and looking forward to it.

The Cookout

It was a gorgeous evening. Carmen and Julie had gone for a swim while Luke was firing up the barbecue and I was making a mixed green salad with fresh tomatoes, shaved corn, mushrooms and avocado with a tangy lime vinaigrette. Moe was doing the bar chores and had a large bucket of cold beers and a pitcher of margaritas ready to go.

Carmen, who had changed out of her wet swimsuit into a pale yellow sundress, took a position up by the bar so she and Moe could discuss the bathing suit prototype that she had been working on. They decided that maybe they could persuade Chris to try it on so they could get a better idea of its functionality.

Lily came out her back door wearing a floor-length, tie-dyed muumuu with dangly turquoise earrings. She looked like an African queen and I'm not referring to the old boat.

The Goddess stepped out of her back porch, elegant in black capris and a strapless black tube top. Her blonde hair was tied loosely back in a ponytail that offset long silver earrings.

"Where's Chris?" Moe asked.

"He'll be along soon," The Goddess said, giving her ponytail a shake.

"Maybe he's inside touching up his mascara," Carmen said.

"Be nice, sis," I said half seriously.

"Tell that boy to get over here," Moe said. "Carmen, go in and grab that prototype. I think that's your phone I hear ringing anyway."

82

Fifteen minutes later, Carmen appeared with the two-piece suit in her hands and a grin on her face. Salt and Pepper followed her out the door, which made a contented Sue lift her head and take note before going back to sleep at the foot of Julie's chaise.

Luke had selected some of Lily's CDs and Lena Horne was singing her heart out.

The mouth-watering aroma of sizzling steaks, chicken breasts and hamburgers was starting to make me hungry. It wasn't Charo, but it was a good effort on all our parts.

"Hey everybody, I've got some news," Carmen said over Lena's rendition of "Fool on the Hill."

"That was Micha. Frank's proposed and they were asking if they could have the ceremony and reception out here by the pool. Luke, Frank wants you to call him when you get a moment. I'm sure he wants you to be his best man."

As if on cue, Lena broke into "Frankie and Johnnie" and everyone laughed. Luke smiled.

"Well, I'll be," Luke said. "Who would have thought those two would be such a terrific match?"

"I'll have to get started on the wedding preparations immediately," Carmen said, eager for the assignment that would involve her organizational and creative skills.

"Hey Carmen, first let's all have a look at that bathing suit," Moe said.

By now Chris had joined us in a tight tank top, cut offs and sandals. There was not much left to the imagination in this getup.

Julie, who loved fashion, got up from her chaise and went over toward Moe and Carmen. She fingered the prototype's fabric, held both the bra and pants up to the fading light and gave a thumbs-up.

We decided to hold off on the modeling because the food was ready and everyone was eager to eat and talk about the impending nuptials.

Carmen was wetting her pants thinking about how she would redecorate her unit and what she would do with all the extra space now that Micha was history. She loved Micha but wanted her space back.

The Goddess wondered if there wasn't a gown in Honey's closet that with a bit of altering would work perfectly for Micha.

Julie expressed that might be a little too trashy for a religious ceremony, but after some consideration, we all agreed that "trashy" was Heave's middle name.

Carmen offered that because of the desert heat it would definitely have to be an evening ceremony and if need be they could use The Way of the Cross if it was simply too hot.

How to handle the Honey situation was another hot topic. Of course Lenny, the maggot, was not welcome but how we could get Honey away from him for an evening was another challenge. Maybe the idea of having two ex-law enforcement officers present might dampen his enthusiasm, but he was such a dumb shit that we all agreed he likely wouldn't pick up on that.

"I don't know if Lenny heard what I whispered in his hairy ear or not the last time I saw him," Luke said.

"Something we don't know?" I said.

Luke cleared his throat.

"I told him that if I ever saw his sorry ass around any of us again, I was going to hit him so hard it would kill his entire family."

"How'd you ever find such a gentle man?" Lily said as she reached down to stroke Beau, who was curled up at her feet, behind the ears.

"Luke Washington, that's some threat," I said.

"I think it's from some movie. Maybe *Diner*. Always seemed to work before, but with that dickweed Lenny you never know what might stick." Luke said.

"Here's my favorite," Chris said. "How would you like to have a handicap spot for the rest of your life?"

"I like that a lot," Luke said.

I frowned.

Some of us were on our second and third drinks and everyone was raving about Chef Washington's culinary skills.

I had stuck to one beer, one chicken breast and lots of salad. I contemplated heading over to The Way of the Cross to work it off, but it was just too glorious a night.

The stars were now out and the twinkle lights around the palm trees cast a soft glow over the pool deck.

Sue had long ago figured out that no more hamburger or steak would be coming her way and had gone back into Julie's.

Mr. Silverman had bravely taken her place and was sharing a chaise with Luke and me.

"I don't know if I should be jealous of this cat or what?" Luke said. His arm was snugly around me as we lay back in the chaise and blessed ourselves for being alive and together on this wonderful night.

Mr. Silverman's engine was running full speed.

We decided it was getting too dark for a fashion show. The Goddess and Chris had said good night what with gymnastics ahead and The Goddess having to go to work in the morning, it was best to postpone.

We three were the only ones left at the pool. Lena had launched into my favorite song, "Rainy Day," and I knew in my heart that this was one of those magic moments in life that I would remember forever.

A jug of wine, a loaf of bread and these two guys beside me in the desert.

She's Home

Charo was in the backseat of Luke's Jaguar begging him to turn down the convertible top and turn up the sound of Marcus Roberts' rendition of "Someone to Watch Over Me." She also reiterated that she felt like going to Teresa's for some spicy Mexican food.

It was great to see her so happy, but I was concerned she was going to overdo it and told her that Carmen had been cooking all morning for her and would be disappointed if she didn't get home soon.

Plus, Sam was arriving tomorrow and she needed to feel her best.

Luke had called Frank while we were waiting to get Charo released from the hospital. Frank, of course, wanted Luke to be his best man and was hoping that we could have the wedding in two weeks. Micha was planning to come back to Carmen's over the weekend so she could work on the preparations. She would bunk with Carmen until the wedding.

Carmen could forget that "Free at Last Speech" she had been chanting.

When we arrived at Heave, Charo couldn't wait to get into her unit. Carmen was there with the table set for two, which was just fine with Luke and me.

We kissed Charo goodbye and told her to get some rest.

Back at my place I went into the kitchen and started to make lunch. I popped open two Sam Adams Lights and began putting together some turkey, tomato and lettuce sandwiches on whole wheat toast with dill pickles and potato chips.

I kept hearing a tiny sound at my back screen door and finally went to investigate.

"I'll be damned," I said. "Ms. Early has something to tell us."

Luke came over to the screen door and looked down at the bird and then looked at me.

"I don't hear a thing," he said.

"You gotta know the signals," I said.

"Is this a code I need to break?"

"Don't be smart. She's telling us Slinky is on her way home from New York and don't ask me how I know this. Animals sense this stuff."

I tore a piece of toast into small pieces and Ms. Early ate this buffet out of my hand. I knew Julie had been keeping Slinky's bird feeder stocked while she was away, but this was an unexpected treat.

I set our lunch out on the kitchen table and told Luke that Ms. Early wasn't the only one who was sensing things.

"What's up? I can tell you have something on your mind."

"Babe, I need to head back to LA today. Got to finish up some business, but you know I'll be back soon for the big wedding. Why don't you come with me?"

"I have some writing I need to complete for a new client, so heading out with you, Buttercup, is tempting but not plausible. Not to mention all the madness that's going to go down here until the nuptials are over. Do you know that this is the first wedding we've ever had at Heave and it likely will be the last."

"Maebeth, my dear, I wouldn't be so sure of that."

Doesn't he know about my commitment condition?

There was a knock on the door and it was Carmen.

"You'll never believe this," she said placing an index card on the kitchen table. "I just finished lunch with Charo and before she went off to rest she dropped this on me saying that she definitely would be baking the wedding cake. She said it was a mix so it wouldn't tire her out if that's what we all were worried about. Christ, this is a disaster. I don't want to hurt her feelings, but this won't do."

Almost Better Than Sex Cake

1 pkg. German chocolate cake mix

1 can Eaglebrand Sweet & Condensed Milk

1 jar (12 oz.) butterscotch caramel topping

1 small container Cool Whip

3 Heath Bars, crushed

Bake cake as directed in a 9x13 inch pan. While still warm, poke holes with handle end of wooded spoon. Mix the milk and topping and pour over cake. Spread Cool Whip over all. Sprinkle crushed candy on top. Refrigerate. Cut into small squares (very rich).

Note: Can be made the day ahead.

"Jesus, Carmen, my arteries are clogging just reading this. Let's let Sam talk her out of this when he gets here," I said.

She nodded.

Luke smiled and was shaking his head as he went into the bedroom to gather up his things.

This was going to be some wedding.

Sam arrived around 11:00 a.m. He had rented an Escalade and had loaded it with groceries and gifts.

Charo was beaming as she introduced him to everyone. You would never know they were related. Sam was big. He was about 6'4" and looked like he liked to eat. He had to use both Charo's and Carmen's refrigerators to hold all his groceries. Carmen was enchanted with the delicacies he'd purchased. These two were going to have fun.

I took Sam over to Monistat 1 to get him settled in.

Sam looked at the suite, stopped cold and stared. His career was in interior design and I readied myself for what was sure to come.

"Oh honnnneeeey, this is the bomb. I love what you've done to this place."

"Sam, I can take it, tell me the truth."

"No, I'm serious, it's so, so Heave," he gushed.

"Let me unpack and then I'll whip up some strawberry pies. Found the cutest fruit and vegetable stand on the way here. The galley kitchen will work fine. I'll get some pie dishes from Gram's and get this going.

On the way back to my place, I yelled through Carmen's screen door, "Sam's making strawberry pies from scratch."

Carmen shot out of her eco chaise like a rocket and was out the door and headed to Monistat 1.

I Do

It was a beautiful sunny Saturday morning. Everyone was back home and excited for today was the big wedding.

Carmen and Sam were poolside going over the list of things yet to be done. I have never seen her so happy and in her element. These two were soulmates. It was to be an early evening wedding and the two were like generals embarking on a battle.

Lily, Slinky and I were over at Charo's having a cup of coffee and talking about the big day. Julie was doing laps in the pool, while Sue kept up with her pace running up and down the length of the pool on the deck. Beau was on a pool chaise sound asleep on his back, legs up and privates pointing skyward.

Luke and Frank were to arrive sometime mid-afternoon keeping alive the tradition that it would be bad luck to see the bride before the wedding. Personally, I had bad luck about every time I saw Micha, but hey, that's just me.

"Christ, Honey's back," I said. "Has anyone seen her? Her car is parked in front of her unit. She must have pulled in late last night."

"How's her big Bonnie and Clyde love affair?" Slinky asked. She had lost track of this soap opera while she luckily had escaped to sane New York.

"I bet they have some damn good sex," Charo said as she stood at the kitchen counter pounding Heath bars into crumbs. "Remember that Brad Pitt in *Thelma and Louise*? That's kinda what I'd like to think is going on between them two."

We had decided to let Charo go ahead with the cake but did have a backup

90

that Sam and Carmen had ordered. It was to be the only outside food that would be brought in since the two gourmets had opted to prepare the food for the wedding.

"Holy shit, check this out," I gasped as I rushed to the kitchen door.

Slinky was right behind me with her hand clasped tightly over her mouth.

Lily, kept repeating, "Oh lawdy, oh lawdy, oh lawdy. Heaven save me."

It was Chris who had emerged from The Goddess' back door wearing the leather-like prototype. He was a vision.

Julie was oblivious and continued with her laps. Carmen and Sam just stood there with their mouths wide open. Even Sue stopped short.

"Good morning," said Chris. "Thought I'd catch a few rays so I would have some color for the big night."

Just then Julie stopped mid-stroke. "Somebody call Moe, right now," she said.

Sam walked over to Chris and introduced himself.

Carmen nodded approval of the prototype, then rolled her eyes, threw the clipboard on an empty chaise and stormed into her unit. Her focus had been broken.

Lily, Slinky and I were now poolside. Charo said there wasn't anything there she hadn't seen before and continued baking.

"Could one of you ladies please oblige and smear some suntan lotion on my back," Chris said.

It was Stonehenge. Nobody moved.

Sam stepped forward.

Soon Sam and Chris were deep in discussion about what we could hardly guess.

It felt good to have a man in residence.

I decided to head over to Honey's and add to the day's drama.

It was early and already this was going to be a day to remember.

Couple of light taps on her back door and Honey appeared. We had made it clear that she would be welcome at the wedding sans Lenny. We also invited her to sing at the ceremony and that was all it took, for Honey loved an audience so much so that now she had branched out and was entertaining at funerals where she was a huge hit.

"Maebeth, so good to see you darling. You're looking great. I hope you're okay with my being here."

Honey had that entertainer's gift of flattery. I had put on some weight since the money-exchange fiasco, but she was too sweet to acknowledge the fact.

On the other hand, Honey had lost weight and looked drawn. Life with her two-bit gangster ex-husband must not be so great.

We sat down in the living room and I could see she was putting on a good front.

"What will you be singing tonight or is a secret?"

"Oh, Carmen has insisted that everything be a surprise so I really can't reveal anything," Honey said."

"Did you see what Chris is wearing?" I said trying to change the subject. "Come on out to the pool and check this out."

We got up from the couch and went out to the pool. Honey took one look and doubled up laughing.

This was so good to hear. This poor soul had been beaten down and to hear her laugh like this brought tears to my eyes. I put my arms around her and tucked her head against my ruby earring. I patted her hair and whispered, "Honey, I will always be here for you. Always."

The Wedding

Out-of-town guests had been told the ceremony started at 4:30 p.m., but they started to arrive early. Micha's daughter, Esther, had arrived and was over at Carmen's with the bride.

Luke and Frank were at my place.

Sam and Carmen were putting the finishing touches around the pool and it looked lovely. White chairs had been lined up on the pool deck and bougainvillea petals were strewn on the aisle down the center. A buffet had been set up outside of The Way of the Cross. Small tables covered with white cloths and colorful fresh flower centerpieces were scattered throughout.

Frank's two sons were expected anytime. They were driving in from Inglewood.

"I'm as nervous as a whore in church," Frank said.

Luke grinned and put his arm around him.

"Aw Frank, it isn't like this is the first time you've made the trip down the aisle," Luke said.

"You think that this would get easier. Jesus, what was I thinking?"

"Maybe you were thinking about sprucing up this chapter of your life," I added.

"Christ, Maebeth, what's wrong with shacking up?" Frank said.

"Too late for that now, stud," I said.

Honey came in and asked me to zip up her gown. She was in lavender with enough of her girls showing to get the guys' attention.

As Honey was leaving, Frank's boys arrived.

They high-fived their dad and then there were big hugs and pats on the back. Both were in their twenties and quite handsome.

I went into the bedroom to change and Luke followed.

"Babe, you are looking so good."

"What are you, Hugh Hefner? Grab a magazine or turn on the TV, I need to concentrate."

I had selected a simple pale pink, long linen dress. I needed to fix the makeup, fasten some combs in the hair and get rolling or Carmen would be pissed.

As I was getting into my dress, Luke came up from behind and kissed the back of my neck.

"Always had a thing for cotton candy," he said.

"Buttercup, that's not exactly the look I was going for."

I turned to look at him and caught my breath. While I was in the bathroom he had changed into a gray pinstripe suit, white shirt and a beautiful silver gray tie.

"You clean up good. God, you are so damn good looking," I said. "We better hit the road before there's trouble and we're late. Besides, Frank and the boys are out there."

He laughed.

Luke went into the living room and I left to help Carmen and Sam.

"Jesus, now what?" Carmen asked as I walked into her unit.

"Just thought you might need an extra hand. Anything I can help you two with?" I asked.

"Okay, go check on Micha in the bedroom. She's in there with Esther," Carmen said.

I opened the bedroom door and there was Micha in a bright red satin, long cocktail dress, chandelier rhinestone earrings and a rhinestone tiara that her daughter was hooking into her hair.

"Was that Honey's gown?" I asked.

"You betcha," Micha said. "I added this tulle around the bodice because I didn't want to be too over the top."

I nodded.

"Good idea, Micha. Frank's boys got here and were almost ready to start the ceremony," I said.

"Maebeth, could you please check on Sam in Monistat 1?

He should be in there with the priest. And is Honey all set with the music? I saw where they delivered a keyboard earlier," Micha said.

"Okay, you look beautiful and this will be a great wedding," I said with my fingers crossed behind my back.

Sam and the clergy were having Jack Daniel's on the rocks when I walked into Monistat 1.

"Yo Maebeth, meet Father Martin. The food is ready to go on the buffet tables immediately after the ceremony. The bar is already set up and Chris and Moe are doing the honors. Seems like they have a lot to discuss. How about a little something to whet your whistle while we wait?" Sam said.

I grinned.

"Why hell, why not? How about a glass of merlot with ice?"

"Coming right up and by the way, that dress is the bomb. Love the simple lines and linen is so, you know, right," Sam said. "Plus, I've only seen you in your running shoes or flip flops and those strappy sandals *sing*, girl."

I wasn't sure what persuasion Sam was, but I liked him more and more every time I was around him.

"Sam, I'm so glad you could extend your visit with Charo. We couldn't have done this without you. It's meant so much to all of us here at Heave," I said.

"Well, I'm having a great time," Sam said refilling his and Father Martin's glasses and handing me my merlot. "In fact, I haven't had a vacation in so long that I'm thinking about staying a little longer if you'll have me."

"Charo will be delighted as will Carmen and all the rest of us," I said.

Father Martin checked his watch and hiccupped.

At Last

The pool area was a fairyland with garlands of soft twinkle lights, fragrant flowers and white candles on the damask covered tables. Moe and Chris had set up their station and were sipping on I don't know what.

Honey was standing by her accompanist, the keyboard player, looking gorgeous.

Guests were starting to file in. The Goddess was greeting everyone and magnificent in kind of a see-through sage chiffon. Julie and Sue were already seated next to Slinky. Lily and Beau were decked out in matching gold lame outfits. Charo was over by the cake table comparing her Almost Better than Sex concoction with the bakery's three-tiered effort. Even Mr. Silverman, curious as ever, was lurking in the flowerbed by Carmen's unit. Frank's boys and Esther were sitting together and getting acquainted.

Honey signaled the keyboard player.

Sam and Carmen took their seats, as did Moe and Chris as the music began.

The keyboard player had some kind of elevator music going, but I knew the best was yet to come. As if on cue, the music changed and Frank and Luke came out of my unit and walked down the bougainvillea-strewn aisle to Honey singing "Our Love is Here to Stay."

This had to be the best looking man I'd ever seen and I'm not talking about Frank.

Maebeth, get hold of yourself. You're pushing 60 and all you want to do is rip this hunk's clothes off. Could it just be that glass of merlot?

After the song, Honey launched into "I Only Have Eyes for You."

What a magnificent voice she had and there wasn't a dry eye in the place. I had goosebumps.

There was a pause of a few minutes and then the keyboard player began "The Wedding March."

Micha appeared with Carmen by her side. Micha looked like a Miss Universe candidate, but Carmen offset the dazzle with her ever-so-correct taupe linen ensemble and chocolate accessories.

These two old friends had been through a lot together.

They strolled up the aisle toward Father Martin who was looking ever so happy.

Frank was beaming. The music stopped as Micha stood by his side smiling.

Father Martin began.

"Micha Skvarika, do you take...Frank Sellars, do you take..."

After the "I do's," Moe yelled "Mazel Tov" and the rest of us chimed in.

Micha and Frank kissed.

Suddenly Gene Autry crooning "I'm Back in the Saddle Again" was blasting from a boombox that had appeared on the cake table. Everyone looked innocent and everyone was hysterical with the exception of Carmen who said, "Oh shit."

The Day After

When I awakened Sunday morning, my head was pounding. Too much merlot. Luke was still asleep so I grabbed fresh clothes and tiptoed into the bathroom for a quick shower.

In the kitchen I poured a glass of tomato juice and laced up my running shoes. I could see out the window that there was major cleaning up that needed to be done at the pool, but I needed to sweat out the vino and go for a run.

I left Luke a note on the kitchen table to tell him I had hit the road.

Heave was quiet. It looked like even Charo, the early bird, was still in bed.

Micha and Frank had stayed overnight at a Ramada Inn in Palm Springs so they could be close to the airport for their honeymoon departure to Cancun. We were less than 100 miles from Mexicali, but I guess they just couldn't get enough of those margaritas and mariachis.

"Oh, my sweet baby," I said as I saw Mr. Silverman sacked out on the front porch. I left the door ajar so he could go in and keep Luke company when he woke up. It wasn't the pussy he probably had been counting on, but it would have to do.

I tore off down the road. Today's carefully chosen purple tee had *You Had Me at Merlot!* stenciled in white on the front. It kind of looked right with the ratty denim cutoffs I had chosen.

It wasn't long before I was in the zone and dripping with sweat.

When I reached The Crossings, I went into the general store for a bottle of water. Then I parked it on a stoop by the gas pump for a rest before I headed back.

Lumbering up the road was a familiar fantastic body. Luke was not clipping along at his usual pace, but it would be hard for him not to look good at any time.

"Buy you a drink, pretty boy?" I said.

"Babe, I was feeling a little shaky this morning and thought how kind and intuitive of you to wake me up with a gentle kiss, when I smelled cat breath," Luke said bending over with his hands on his knees trying to catch his breath.

"Buttercup, I don't see how you could do much better than Mr. Silverman."

"Maybe you're right, but he's not really my type. I kinda go for the well-dressed athlete," Luke said giving me the once over.

"You know, hot stuff, I do love sex and once was told that the only time I ever said "NO" was when I didn't understand the question. However, today may be a first because I'm a little hung over and see a big pool clean up in my near future."

"Well, let me introduce a thought while you're in a weak state. Let's get Heave cleaned up, kick back the rest of the day and then the first thing tomorrow I want to grab you and very few of your clothes and take you back to my home in Malibu."

"What? I can't just take up and leave."

Luke smiled.

"Maebeth, what's keeping you? Let the Heave girls work out their own problems. Carmen can feed Mr. Silverman and you and I can spend some time together in a different environment. Besides, I don't intend to ever let you go so step into my world for a while."

He's right. What's with me and commitment?

We huffed and puffed our way back to Heave with little breath to spare for talk.

Carmen, Slinky, Lily, Julie and The Goddess were out at the pool tidying up.

Moe and Chris were sunbathing and Moe had a pad on top of a copy of *Gentlemen's Quarterly* taking notes, I assumed on Chris' two-piece attire.

"Where's Charo?" I asked.

"She's in with Sam making some breakfast for everyone," Carmen said.

"It's like someone had an orgy out here," Slinky said.

"Hey, Moe and Chris, don't wear yourself out over there," I yelled.

"We'll be fine as soon as we get our coffee," Moe said.

Was it their mothers who made such invalids out of men? Or were they just natural-born jerks?

I grabbed a trash bag and started stuffing it with napkins, cigar butts and plastic water bottles.

Slinky was hosing down the deck while Carmen and Lily were wiping down the furniture. Julie was skimming out the pool with a long net. The Goddess was dismantling the catering tables and in all we were making decent progress.

"Anybody for some grub?" Luke yelled, while walking out of Charo's with a pot of coffee and a stack of styrofoam cups.

"What's with the styrofoam?" Carmen said.

"Let's ignore sis for a minute," I said.

"Come on in and help yourself to Gram's Chiles Rellenos," Sam said. "It's the ole hair of the dog and we've got a big pitcher of Bloody Marys to keep the heat down."

"Hot damn," Luke said.

"Works for me," Moe said getting up from the chaise.

"Anybody have some deli turkey, lettuce, no mayo on wheat? That's what I'd like," The Goddess said.

I shook my head.

"Let me start with a celery stalk in the Bloody Mary," I said.

Charo was bustling about the kitchen beaming. She had her Sam by her side along with a slew of healthy appetites. It was so great seeing her back to her old self again.

Chris shoveled Chile Rellenos onto his plate and parked out by the pool to work on his tan.

Carmen ran into her unit to fetch a turkey on whole wheat, lettuce, tomato, no mayo and a few chips and dill slices for The Goddess.

Ms. Early was perched on Slinky's shoulder not wanting to miss a nibble.

Sue and Beau were on the alert for any crumbs.

Lily's svelte frame was snake-coiled on a chaise patting Beau's head and nursing a Bloody Mary. "Oh those chiles are takin' the pain for a fine ride," she said.

Luke had his arm around Charo and was whispering who-knows-what into her ear.

She stood on her tiptoes to kiss him on the cheek.

"Hot damn, you'll have the recipe first thing this afternoon," Charo said.

Everyone froze as Honey ran out of her unit followed by Lenny.

I could adjust to Malibu.

Drama

"Will someone please tell this fuckin' rat bastard that I'm not going with him?" Honey shouted.

It was a religious tableau with Moses (my Luke) getting up ever so slowly and walking toward Honey and Lenny.

We could hardly hear him ask Honey if she preferred staying at Heave. I felt a cold shiver at this side of Luke that I'd only seen a few times before.

Luke walked over to Lenny and no one could hear what he said. The energy was electric and even, or especially, the animals were restless.

Without a word, Lenny turned on his heel and stormed out of the pool area and into Honey's unit. Luke paused and then followed him. In what seemed like forever we heard a bike rev up and head into the desert.

"Are there any more Chiles Rellenos?" Luke said as he exited Honey's unit and headed for Charo's.

I nodded.

After everyone resumed chewing, Honey came over and sat down next to me and The Goddess.

"You've got to dump this loser," The Goddess said.

"Honey, this isn't going to get any better," I added.

"I know, I know. I'm through with this guy. What was I thinking? I want to stay here at Heave and never see that creep again," Honey said.

Luke joined us and told her that she should consider a restraining order.

Honey sighed and headed toward Charo's for some breakfast.

Julie and Carmen were doing laps in the pool.

Slinky said she was tired and went inside.

Lily and Sam were helping Charo clean up.

I headed back to my place for a shower.

I was dressed and feeling almost human when Luke walked in.

"What in the world did you say to Lenny?"

"I just explained that this was the second time I told him to beat it and if there was ever a third time, I didn't think he would enjoy it and maybe he could leave a list of next of kin to notify with Honey."

"God, you're sexy when you go into that stealth mode."

"Babe, if that's what does it for you, I'll just shut up and act quiet."

"Come here," I said patting the couch. "I want to talk about us."

"Uh-oh Maebeth, this scares me a hell of a lot more than Lenny."

"Okay, relax, I've been thinking a short visit to Malibu might be a good thing. In fact, I'm excited about seeing how you live and getting to see another side of you. I know I'm not big on plans, commitments and whatever, but you are too exquisite to throw back in the pond."

"Whew," Luke said.

There was a knock on the front door and it was Charo. Luke let her in and she handed him her recipe.

Luke bowed and kissed her hand.

Chiles Rellenos

1 4-oz. can sweet green chiles
2 eggs, separated
2 tbsp flour
Flour for coating chiles
Sharp Cheddar cheese

Oil for deep frying

Remove ribs and seeds from chiles. Place a piece of cheese in each chile. Beat egg yolks slightly. Beat egg whites until they hold a soft peak. Gently fold the yolks into the whites. Fold in flour. Heat the oil to about 400 degrees. Roll cheese-stuffed chiles in flour. Then with a large spoon dip chiles into the batter, coating generously. Place in hot oil and fry until brown, 3 to 4 minutes. (Instead of dipping, I put a spoonful of butter in the oil, lay the chile on that, then put another spoonful of butter on top of the chile.)

Sauce

1 14-oz. can of stewed tomatoes

2 tbsp finely chopped onions

½ tsp salt

½ tsp oregano

Pepper to taste

Mix all ingredients in a saucepan and simmer 10 minutes.

Serve over Chiles Rellenos.

"Sit down and join us, Charo," Luke said. "Maebeth was just telling me how terrific I am."

"Well, she is right on," Charo said. "It's good to see Maebeth with a little color in her cheeks from something else besides jogging. We love Maebeth and we love that you've made her so happy. I mean what is that saying? A hard man is good to find."

"Now I'm blushing," Luke said.

"How's Lester?" I asked trying to change the subject.

"Maebeth, he's a good man. Notice how I left out the hard part," Charo said with her eyes twinkling. "At my age I just want them continent. Is that too much to ask?"

"Oh God, look what I have to look forward to," I said.

Gotta Go

It was another beautiful morning. The sky was streaked pink and there was a slight breeze. Summer was coming to an end and the days and nights were getting cooler.

Yesterday had been fun. We watched *Harold and Maude* and *Wedding Crashers* and spent the day making popcorn and love.

I laced up my running shoes and headed out while Luke slept. My mind was racing about the trip to Malibu. What should I bring? Who were his friends? How did he live? Actually, I knew very little about him and I could say that I haven't told him my complete life story. What I did know was that he was easy and fun to be around. I was also proud to be seen with him. And even better, all my fellow Heave friends adored him.

On the way back I bumped into Luke who had just started his run.

"Take your time, Buttercup. I need some time to figure out what to take from my vast wardrobe."

Luke grinned.

"Pack light, Babe."

Back at Heave, I went over to check on Charo. She was having coffee on her porch and invited me to sit down and chat.

Coffee sounded great and I stretched out on her glider and enjoyed the morning.

Sam would be heading back to New York tomorrow. It had been a wonderful visit and Charo would miss him.

"I think Carmen is going to miss Sam a lot. They really hit it off," I said.

"Maebeth, those two have so much in common. Sam's already invited Carmen to New York to see some plays."

I finished my coffee, kissed Charo goodbye and walked over to Slinky's to check on her. She had been looking tired lately.

"Slinky, it's Maebeth, you up?"

Slinky came to the door, exotic as ever in a long, emerald green, silk robe.

"Hi Maebeth, come on in. I hear you're going to Malibu for a few days. It will do you good to get out of here."

"Just wanted to see how you were feeling," I said.

"I've been awfully tired lately. Ever since I got back from New York I can't seem to get my old energy back. I'm seeing a doctor this week," Slinky said.

"Well, you have my cell phone number if you want to talk about anything," I said.

"You're such a little mother to all of us. Between you and Charo we're all pretty well taken care of."

"How's Jack?" I asked.

"He's been traveling a lot, but I expect he'll be out here in a couple weeks. I miss this guy even when I'm with him, but it just works better with us on both coasts," Slinky said.

"Well, I need to start packing. I'm a little nervous about this whole trip. Do you think I'm making the right decision? I mean I'm worried about Honey and I haven't really had time to get myself mentally prepared for this trip."

"Now Maebeth, what ever happened to that adventurous girl I met in Rome? You're not going to China and you and Luke really seem to be so perfect for each other. This trip will do you good."

"You are so right," I said putting my arm around Slinky's shoulder and giving her a kiss on the cheek. "Take care and call me and let me know what the doctor has to say."

Slinky nodded.

I headed out to the pool where Julie and Carmen were doing laps. Sam was stretched out on a chaise reading the *Los Angeles Times*.

I said my goodbyes and headed home. Luke was already back and decided to wash his car and gas up at The Crossings while I was getting ready.

I started pulling clothes out of my closet and heard a knock on my door. It was The Goddess. When she saw what I was doing, she put her hands on her hips and let out a huge sigh.

"Thank God I dropped by. Maebeth, you are going to Malibu. You are leaving Sleepy Hollow. Get a grip."

"Beam me up Scotty. I welcome the help."

"For starters, you are not taking any of those tees. Look what you're wearing, that tee with *Grow Your Own Dope—Plant a Man*. Personally, I don't think that's right for anywhere."

"Goddess dear, these are my trademark. Next to my grandma's ruby earrings, this collection is my second most favorite treasure. Don't you think a girl needs to make a statement every now and then?"

The Goddess ignored me.

I sat on the bed and watched her tear through my closet.

"Okay, this long black jersey dress is a keeper. And this gray shawl with the silver fringe looks great with it. Alright, you're taking these strappy black heels."

"Those suckers kill me. What about my running shoes?"

The Goddess ignored me.

"Now, the right fitting jeans are good with a lacy camisole. These Teva sandals are fine. Look at all these Eccos and Clark's. I can't believe someone actually had sex with you what with the way you dress."

"Hey, I have some podiatry issues," I said.

"You do have a few decent velour warm-up outfits. And this long brown skirt with that big beige pullover and the big leather belt work. What about nightgowns?"

"Those would be these extra large tees. Very comfy."

"This really frightens me," The Goddess said. "I'm going back to my place to grab a few things. You have got to keep a man interested and you're dressing like someone a man might like to go deer hunting with."

"You know I couldn't kill an animal," I said.

The Goddess glared at me and left.

She returned with a black peignoir set, velvet slippers, a couple of cashmere pullovers to wear with the jeans and a pair of snakeskin cowgirl boots.

Everything fit and I had to admit I was looking pretty hot as she coordinated the outfits.

I pulled on a pair of jeans and a big white linen shirt over an Adam & Eve white t-shirt that had been a birthday gift from Carmen. Slipped on some beige ropy wedgies and was ready to roll.

Look out Malibu.

Luke chuckled when he saw the suitcases sitting by the front door.

"Babe, I was suggesting a visit, but if you want to move in, it's fine with me."

"Smart mouth, Buttercup, I'm going to say goodbye to Honey and Lily and then we can be on our way."

Honey was just out of bed and looked hungover and worried. She hadn't heard from Lenny, but she knew he wasn't out of the picture. I gave her a hug and walked over to Lily's.

Lily was excited for me. She told me to remember every detail and to call her as often as I could.

"Jesus, Lily, I'll only be gone a few days. Everyone's acting like I'm going to the moon."

Next I stopped by Carmen's to make sure she knew exactly what to do with

Mr. Silverman. He would be happier on his own turf, but she would need to check up on him and let him out at night and back in the morning.

Carmen had packed some sandwiches, chips, pickles, brownies and a thermos of lemonade in a basket for our road trip.

I gave her a big hug and kiss.

"Goodbye sister, have a wonderful time," Carmen said with tears in her eyes.

Note to travel agent: Get my ass out of here more often.

The Journey

We were on the PCH and the twisting terrain as we headed into Malibu made my stomach sink.

Luke had been the perfect tour guide pointing out his favorite places and giving me a little history along the way. This was the same stretch infamously popularized by bad boys Nick Nolte, Robert Downey Jr. and Mel Gibson.

I could see and smell the ocean and felt like a young girl eager to experience new things with someone I was crazy about. I was also concerned that once out of my element things between us might change.

Maybe everything won't be so peachy once I get to really know him or worse yet, when he gets to know me.

Luke pulled into a narrow driveway and popped open the garage door. He said he'd get the luggage later and led me up a steep stairs to his gorgeous architectural wood and glass beach home. A huge porch fronted the home which looked out over the Pacific. The crashing waves, glistening sand and hungry pelicans overwhelmed me. There must be at least 50 feet of beach frontage.

The entire front of the home was glass. Teak tables and chaises with nautical blue and white stripes looked out over the surf. A sleek barbecue and a small refrigerator were tucked to the side.

Luke fumbled for his house key, pushed back the slider and turned to face me. "Ms. Caletti, may I have the honor?" he said as he scooped me into his arms and crossed the threshold.

His housekeeper had already been there because windows were open letting the fresh sea breezes in and there was a chilled bottle of champagne in a silver ice bucket on the bar.

The furnishings were exquisitely minimalistic. Lots of rich black leather, glass, chrome and oriental carpets on pale travertine floors.

"Luke, this is amazing," I said as he gently put me down. I could tell that he was proud of his home. "To think I put you up in Monistat 1 when you were accustomed to these digs."

"Babe, I got accustomed to you and an igloo or tent would do as long as you're with me. Let me fix us some champagne and then we'll continue the tour. Actually by Malibu standards, this is a bit of a bungalow, but I've lived here for more than 20 years and I've never gotten tired of it."

We sipped champagne from what looked like Waterford flutes and Luke showed me his office which was very impressive with a huge mahogany desk, the very latest computer equipment and miles of bookshelves stocked with books you could tell weren't props. There was a guest bedroom oddly feminine with chintz wallpaper, brass queen headboard and billowy French lace curtains. There were three full baths and a powder room off the living room. A den sported the largest plasma screen I had ever seen and wonderful over-stuffed couches and ottomans that invited you to plop. The kitchen was knockout complete with Wolf appliances and the very latest of everything including a built-in wok and copper pots hanging over an island butcher block. Off the dining area there was a small wine room.

All so very neat with no clutter whatsoever.

Last was the master bedroom. It was huge and overlooked the water. It boasted a king-size bed with crisp white hotel linen and a powder blue blanket tucked military style. A large fireplace was to the side set among a built-in entertainment center. Beaded curtains led to the porch, which had a litany of wind chimes already in song. Windows in the bedroom rose above the sliders bringing even more of the sky into the room.

Adjacent to the bedroom was a smaller space totally walled in mirrors except for one that let you watch the waves as you worked out. A treadmill, elliptical bike, rowing machine and major weight lifting equipment told me that this extraordinary 60+ year-old body I'd been enjoying was the product of some genetics and lots of hard work.

"Luke, I, for once, am speechless. This is grand and I'm so proud of you. You have made such a success of your life to have warranted such a wonderful home. I'm just so happy for you."

"Well, there's one more big surprise if you can handle it," Luke said.

"Lay it on me."

"I have a daughter. She's been staying next door at my neighbors, Lucy and Mel Bergmann, and I need to get her and bring her home."

Here it all comes. Christ, a daughter. Sure, I have a lot of stuff he doesn't know, but a daughter, Jesus. What's next? About that guest bedroom, now it all figures.

I tried not to look surprised, went back into the living room, poured myself another champagne and walked out to the porch.

In no time at all I heard Luke coming up the stairs. "Okay, honey, I missed you, too. Can't wait 'til you meet my other girl. Here, give daddy another kiss."

I had stretched out on a chaise, closed my eyes which were hidden under large sunglasses and pretended to be dozing. All of a sudden I felt a hot tongue licking my face.

"Meet Miss Daisy," Luke said.

I opened my eyes to a tail-wagging chocolate lab.

Thank you, Jesus.

Paradise

Luke was full of surprises. He had tickets this evening to the Los Angeles Philharmonic's *Fireworks & Tchaikovsky Under the Starry Sky* at the Hollywood Bowl.

His housekeeper had filled his refrigerator with cold cuts, cheeses and coleslaw.

We took a quick nap, ate and got dressed for the evening. Thank god for the black dress and the shawl. Thank god for The Goddess.

Miss Daisy was curled up fast asleep on the den couch.

I felt that I was in another country.

The evening just got better and better. When the USC Trojan Marching Band joined in the finale set to the "1812 Overture," I couldn't recall a happier end-of-summer night.

It was chilly when I awoke the following morning. Luke was gone but he had covered me with a down quilt. My blood was still attuned to the desert climate. I got out of bed wearing one of Luke's tees. Sorry Goddess, the peignoir set was still in my suitcase. I could smell the coffee and headed down the hall toward the kitchen.

After pouring my self a cup of java I started to look for Luke and found him in his office with Miss Daisy at his feet.

"Good morning, Miz Caletti. Miss Daisy and I were about to wake you and ask if you'd care to join us on our morning run. You know, here you are on a beach and you haven't even gotten your toes wet."

"Give me three minutes," I said.

I could tell Miss Daisy and Luke had a routine. She would race ahead and then circle back and then race ahead again.

It was glorious running on the hard-packed sand near the water's edge. There were other runners and their dogs and everyone waved, whistled or said "hello."

I had put on sweats and a tee that I had managed to sneak in the suitcase. It read: *I'm All In*.

We were coming back up on Luke's house, when I slowed it down.

I placed my hand on Luke's arm.

"Could I have a moment, dear man?"

Luke nodded.

I lay down on the sand and made an angel. Luke joined me and Miss Daily thought it was a game.

We sat up and looked out at the water. Luke put one arm around me, the other around his sweet Lab and was silent.

I stared at the surf and the sun coming through a pink sky, turned to Luke and whispered, "Thank you."

Luke swallowed hard and said, "Let's get some breakfast. We can come back here anytime."

"Luke, you are not on vacation and I know you have things you need to do. Please don't let my being here distract you from your work."

"Maebeth, I have been alone for so many years. I can't tell you how wonderful it is to finally have someone to share my life with. I know we have a lot to learn about each other and it's my hope that this time together will give us that chance."

"Okay, I want to tell you all about my sordid past, but first I'm hungry, big boy."

Luke smiled and put his arm around me.

We ate breakfast out on the porch.

Luke cleared his throat and said, "Well, here goes. Many, many years ago I was very much in love with a young woman. She was finishing college at Howard University and I was completing my training in what we shall call clandestine operations. We married after she graduated, but the passion soon waned, thanks to my frequent long absences that I couldn't share with her. I was young and I made a choice and she came in second. I have always felt guilty about it and think the failed marriage and, of course, the job kept me from forming any long-lasting, future relationships. When I met you, everything changed. True, I'm semi-retired and not as driven as I was in my younger days, but everything about you felt right. Call it kismet, karma, chemistry—can't really explain it, but I knew that first night I met you and Lily at Heave that my life had shifted in a major way."

I smiled.

"Did you have any children? I mean besides Miss Daisy."

"No, and I have no regrets. I don't think I would have been much of a father. I had wonderful parents but grew up in the '60s full of idealism and full of myself. It was a very selfish generation."

"You are preaching to the choir on that subject," I said. "I was a bit of a flower child and raging feminist. For me, it was all about freedom. Freedom was power. I had long relationships and a couple of proposals, but the thought of having to give up any of my freedom kept me from the altar. Carmen, on the other hand, got married early, had a kid and a totally different life from mine. You would hardly believe we are sisters. We are so different. As for parents, ours were the best, but our dad got sick and died way too young leaving us with not a lot of anything but each other. That proved to be more than enough because our mother was one sweet, tough Italian lady who took no prisoners. Never really wanted to have kids after I saw how much my mother sacrificed.

She didn't complain, but she had to wonder what her life might have been had she made other choices."

"Okay Babe, so we won't have kids," Luke said with a twinkle in his eye as he got up from the chair and bent down to kiss me lightly on top of my frizzy hairdo.

"Hmmm, can't a girl change her mind? Let's go try."

The Neighbors

It was Tuesday and Luke had invited the Bergmanns over for lunch. I could have used Charo's expertise, but I did know how to cook a few things.

I had scoped out a supermarket in a nearby shopping center and feeling right at home hopped in Luke's infamous truck, which he kept for undercover work. This was the same vehicle that had the mysterious break down the night we first met, so I had a soft spot for it.

The menu would be crusty Italian bread, antipasto salad, Italian Wedding Soup and spumoni ice cream for dessert. A little weird, but everything I loved. Plus, Luke had an extraordinary 18-year-old balsamic vinegar that I would combine with an excellent extra virgin olive oil and a dash of sea salt for dipping.

"Little Miss Homemaker," Luke said standing in the kitchen doorway beaming.

"Ciao, baby."

"My kitchen has never seen such activity and for that matter who knew I had so many pots and pans."

I grinned.

"Buttercup, we got to get you over this neat thing," I said, pushing a strand of hair behind my ear, "and can you hand me the escarole?"

When the Bergmanns arrived, Miss Daisy went nuts. They were equally ballistic about seeing her and I knew why Luke liked them and why he could get away without guilt.

Lucy Bergmann was delightful. A retired professor of English literature, hospice volunteer and avid traveler, she reminded me of a petite version of Slinky with her dark good looks and classic style. She was wearing a loose-fitting tangerine caftan with gold hoop earrings and gold sandals. Her gray hair was cut very short and complemented her aquiline features

Mel had been in the film business. His company actually supplied film to the studios and although he was officially retired, he owned the company and had not totally relinquished the reins. He was a big guy, way beyond balding with an outgoing personality. He had on a Tommy Bahama navy and white shirt over khaki shorts and brown leather Birkenstocks. He looked like he would be comfortable in most any situation.

"It's five o'clock somewhere," Luke said as he opened a bottle of red wine. Although there was also a pitcher of iced tea on the bar, everyone opted for the wine, which certainly didn't taste like the two-buck-Chuck that I was accustomed to.

The Bergmanns were lovely and I caught Luke out of the corner of my eye, giving me an appreciative once-over.

Good lord, I'm pushing 60 and this man is looking at me as if I'm this hot tamale.

Lunch went along smoothly with everyone having a grand time and complimenting me on my gourmet efforts; that is, until I tore off a piece of Italian bread and tried to slip it to Miss Daisy, who knew a patsy when she saw one.

"Absolutely not," Luke said.

I froze.

This could have been our first fight, but I acquiesced and patted his daughter lightly on the head as I palmed the bread into my napkin.

Wars have been initiated on less provocation. We took our dishes of spumoni out onto the porch overlooking the Pacific.

Great people, great day, great life.

After the Bergmanns had said their goodbyes, Luke helped me with the dishes.

"Damn, they loved you Babe, just as I knew they would. You were totally terrific, but I have just a small question. What's with the cowboy boots?"

"Aww shit, Luke, that's the work of The Goddess. She felt I needed to Rodeo Drive-it-up a little. In the desert we tend to get a little too casual and she tried, bless her heart, to chic me up."

"Ride 'em cowgirl," Luke said, grabbing our two glasses of wine and heading for the bedroom.

I followed.

"Aw shucks, pilgrim," I said.

Slinky's in Trouble

My cell phone rang around 9:30 the next morning. It was Carmen and although she was trying to be chatty and ask about my visit, I could tell by her voice that something was off.

"What's up?" I asked.

"It's Slinky," Carmen said. "She had her doctor's appointment yesterday, came home and holed up in her unit. Jack tried calling her from New York, knowing she was seeing the doctor and after not being able to reach you, finally called here. I have no idea what's going on but thought you'd want to know. She's the closest to you so maybe you could give her a call and at least leave her a message if she doesn't pick up. I'm so sorry to bother you, sis, but I knew you'd want to know."

"I don't like the sound of this," I said.

I hung up and dialed Slinky. Got the voice machine.

"Hey, Slinky. It's Maebeth. You were so right. It's great to be here in Malibu. I can't wait to tell you about Luke's home. Anyway, he's working and I'm a little homesick so give me a call if you have a moment."

Ten minutes later Slinky called back.

"Maebeth, got your message. I've been in a grand funk. Fact is, I have colon cancer," Slinky said.

My heart stopped.

"Oh God, no. What about a second opinion?"

"Maebeth, I've done my homework. The cancer is at an advanced stage.

121

I've done a lot of thinking and have decided to forgo chemo. Under the circumstances, I want to make the most out of the time I have left."

"I'm coming home," I said.

"No, I don't want you to," Slinky said.

"Slinky, I respect your wishes but one way or another, I'm going to be with you. Hey, how about if you come here? Luke has to be away on business for a few days and it's just me and Miss Daisy."

"Miss Daisy?"

"Oh, sorry, that's his dog. Anyway we can drink wine, walk along the beach and talk. I want to be with you, Slinky. You gave me good advice about getting out of the desert and expanding my circle. Now, it's my turn. Please Slinky, say 'yes.'"

"You make that sound inviting, Maebeth."

"Great, then it's settled. Okay, I'm going to arrange to have a car drive you here. I'll call you back with the time they'll pick you up. Luke can bring us back to Heave over the weekend. Have you told Jack?"

"I haven't been able to get up the courage. He'll want to be here right away and I really need some time to get my mind around all of this. I will call him and tell him I'm going to the beach. We can discuss what would be the best approach to break the news."

"Maybe you could invite him to Heave for the weekend. You're going to need to tell him," I said.

"You're right. That's a good idea, Maebeth. Thanks. I don't know what I'd do if it weren't for you."

"You'd do fine, my friend. You are the most exceptional woman I have ever known."

We hung up and I sat stone still on the porch overlooking the ocean. Seagulls were chatting it up, the fog was burning off and my world had just turned dark.

I got up from the chaise and went to find Luke. He was in his office glued to the computer screen. I told him about Slinky and my invitation and when he came over to put his arms around me, I broke into sobs.

Luke held me tight.

"I'm so glad you got Slinky to come here. There is something about being by the water that can be so contemplative and soothing. You girls can have a good visit. I'm sure you're exactly what Slinky needs right now."

"I'm not all that strong, Luke. Everyone thinks I have it so together but look at me. I'm a wreck."

"Babe, can you see me sleeping with a wreck?"

Luke went back to work and I went out on the porch to make some calls. First, I arranged for a car service to pick up Slinky the next morning. Next, I called Carmen and filled her in. I told her not to tell anyone else. Spreading the word had to be on Slinky's terms. Then I called Slinky back and left a message that the car service would pick her up a 10:00 a.m. the following day.

Feeling a little wobbly made me think of Honey, so I called her. She picked up on the first ring.

"Were you sitting on top of the phone?" I asked.

"Yeah, I'm a little jumpy. That freakin' Lenny has been threatening me again. He says he wants alimony. Can you believe that asshole? We're not even married anymore, but he says that's what it's going to take for him to back off."

"I thought Luke had scared the beejesus out of him, but guess not," I said. "We are going to have to come up with something that will get through to this mope. I'll be back home this weekend and let's chat then. How's everyone else?"

"Slinky has been very quiet. I hope she's okay," Honey said.

"She going to spend a few days with me here in Malibu. I'll find out what's going on."

It's pretty obvious that we were not going to be able to keep Slinky's condition under wraps for too long.

Best Friends

Luke left early the next morning. We kissed goodbye and he told me that he'd call, to help myself to anything and that he'd be back sometime Friday. He didn't tell me where he was going or give me any details and I didn't ask. His business was a very private matter and I think he was trying to protect me, but not knowing what was going on made me anxious. This was all new and if I was to be part of this duo, I needed to honor his way of operating.

Slinky arrived early afternoon. She looked drawn but yet as beautiful as ever.

We hugged.

"Maebeth, what a pad this is."

"Bachelor pad, you mean."

"Oh, this view! I can't wait to hit the beach," Slinky said.

Miss Daisy nudged her leg.

"This must be the other woman," Slinky said.

"Actually, Miss Daisy is his major love. Although, it's nice she isn't the jealous type."

"Tough competition," Slinky said scratching Miss Daisy between the ears.

Miss Daisy didn't leave her side. Dogs know things.

"Let me take your things and show you your room. I'm still not sure why this guest room is so feminine compared to the rest of this house. That's one mystery that's yet to unfold. How about a glass of chardonnay while I put some lunch together?"

124

"Start pouring," Slinky said.

"Take your time," I said and then wished I hadn't.

She went to freshen up and I poured the wine and took our glasses out to the porch. Slinky joined me having changed into a long, light blue, gauzy skirt, a navy tank top and a pair of silver leather sandals. Silver bangles were stacked on her arms and matched her dangly silver earrings.

"God, this is so beautiful, Maebeth. Luke must be doing very well. There is absolutely no pretense about him, so who would know he had such a fine home."

"I'm so lucky, Slinky. I can't believe how wonderful we are together. I hope I don't discover that he's a mass murderer or something equally awful. Sip your wine and enjoy the view. I'm going to put a little lunch together. We can eat out here."

I had made some chicken salad with green grapes, added some pickles, sliced tomatoes and black olives. We sat at a round teak table on the porch and talked about everything but cancer.

Waving a pickle in her hand with the thin silver bangles glistening on her arm, Slinky said, "Maebeth, I'm okay with all this. I have had a wonderful life. A wonderful marriage, albeit unusual, and I've seen the world many times over. My successful career as a dancer was the fulfillment of a dream I'd had since childhood. I've been blessed. Yes, I might buy a little more time with chemo, but I'd rather feel as good as I can for as long as I can. I know there will be more tears, especially when I think of Jack and of telling my family, but these are the cards I've been dealt."

"You are so brave," I said, my eyes welling with tears.

"Oh Maebeth, it isn't bravery. I have no choice in this matter and I would rather expend my energy taking a last look at everything as opposed to feeling sorry for myself. Just look at that endless water out in front of us and listen to those seagulls. My life here on earth is so insignificant compared to the bigger picture. Death is just another chapter. It's a mystery that I don't know the outcome of, but one that I'm curious about. Don't take me wrong, but I'm kinda looking forward to seeing what and if there's something hereafter. Now promise me that you and I will celebrate life during this visit and the days I have left and let's not dwell on the cancer."

Miss Daisy walked over and sat at her feet.

"You gotta deal, Slinky," I said fighting back the tears. "The sun is starting to go down a bit. How about that walk on the beach?"

Slinky was reveling in the wet sand between her toes when Miss Daisy spotted someone and raced off in front of us.

It was Lucy Bergmann and she bent down to hug Miss Daisy who was acting like she hadn't seen her friend in years.

We approached.

"Lucy Bergmann, meet my dear friend Slinky Rue, who is spending a few days with me while Luke is away."

The two shook hands and got acquainted while Lucy joined us on our walk. I remembered that Lucy was a hospice volunteer and wondered if she might be able to help Slinky in some way. I wasn't quite sure how to approach this when Lucy asked if we had dinner plans. She had just learned that Mel had a last minute business engagement and she had made a seafood casserole with shrimp and crabmeat and it was way too much good food to waste.

"What do you say, Slinky? Are you too tired from your trip or would you like to go?" I said.

"Lucy, that sounds lovely. I would love to join you for dinner," Slinky said.

"I am assuming that Miss Daisy is invited," I said.

Lucy raised an eyebrow as if she couldn't even comprehend the question. The Bergmanns was Miss Daisy's second home.

"Maebeth, Miss Daisy doesn't need an invitation," Lucy said.

We went back to Luke's and Slinky wanted to rest a little before dinner.

Heave

I took a quick shower, put on a terry robe and sat out on the porch to think. The thought that Slinky would no longer be a part of my life was devastating. We had known each other for a long time. This would be Heave's second loss for we all still mourned Charo's Sarah.

A New Friend

The Bergmann home was gorgeous. Not quite as modern as Luke's and a bit of showcase for souvenirs from their world travels.

Slinky, Heave's world traveler, was enchanted with what she saw and Lucy proved to be a terrific tour guide for each object had a wonderful story to go along with it.

After a magnificent meal, Lucy and Slinky cleaned up the kitchen while I took Miss Daisy out for some personal business she had to attend to.

When we returned, the two ladies were deep in conversation. Slinky looked up when she saw us.

"Maebeth, can you believe how things work out? I just learned that Lucy is familiar with hospice and I think it would be extremely helpful if I linked up with a volunteer for the journey I have ahead of me."

"And I am honored to be Slinky's volunteer," Lucy said.

I hugged them both.

Miss Daisy wagged her tail.

On the way back to Luke's, Slinky looked up at the stars and said how blessed she felt to have so many wonderful friends in her life.

"I'm so glad I came over to Malibu. Now I feel as if I can move forward and speak to Jack and my family with confidence. In fact, I think I'll call Jack when we get back to Luke's," Slinky said.

The phone was ringing when we got home. It was Luke. I filled him in on everything. We did a little purring at each other and then I put the phone up to Miss Daisy's ear so he could do a little purring with his main squeeze.

Slinky was on her cell, I assumed talking to Jack.

I got ready for bed and went into the kitchen for a cup of tea.

When Slinky joined me, she looked like a boulder had been lifted from her shoulders.

"How'd it go?" I said.

"It was a lot for Jack to handle, but I think he will be fine. He's a strong guy. And we plan on being together a lot these next few months. He will be coming to Heave on Saturday. I am so glad Luke will be there for him. Nothing like having one of the brothers with you at a time like this."

"Solidarity," I said. Miss Daisy barked in agreement.

Catching Up

The next morning we were up early and on the beach. Both of us were in shorts and tanks and barefoot. Miss Daisy would run ahead of us and return with sticks and anything else she thought we might enjoy.

"Maebeth, I can't tell you how much my talk with Lucy helped. She's an amazing woman and I believe sincerely wants to be by my side. There's something about walking toward this with someone you have no history with. It's like two souls coming together at a place in time. I will call her today and thank her. Hopefully I can find the right words."

"Oh, you will, Slinky. I'm so happy the two of you got together. Speaking of getting together, Luke will be home this evening. Maybe I'll do a little work with the free weights. Got to be in shape for this hunk."

Slinky called Lucy and they decided to get together and talk.

I worked out and then called Honey to see how she was doing.

"Oh, Maebeth, that bastard is after me. I just know something horrible is going to happen. If there was just some treatment this asswipe could get—like a lobotomy or medicine or something," Honey said.

Treatment, did she say treatment? Bingo, I've got it.

"Jesus, Honey, I just got an idea. Do me a favor. Go to the library and get the movie *Reservoir Dogs*. I'll be home tomorrow. Whatever you do, don't mention the movie or anything else about Lenny to Luke or Jack, who will be arriving tomorrow, too. And then set up a Heave conference. Tell the girls it's strictly confidential and we have a lot to cover. Make it for Sunday afternoon

130

around 3:00 p.m. Oh, and tell Julie and The Goddess not to mention anything to Moe or Chris."

Next I called Carmen to bring her up to speed and check on Mr. Silverman. She said she'd heard from Micha and Frank and they were as happy as could be. Carmen went on to extol how marvelous it was to have the place to herself and how she planned to redecorate thanks to some wonderful tips she had gotten from Sam, her new best friend.

I agreed.

Next I touched base with Lily who had been unusually quiet and probably dying to find out every romantic detail of my visit.

"I've been sittin' on my hands so I wouldn't pick up the phone and bug you," Lily said. "How many times you done it since you left?"

"Hey, I've got a girl for Beau," I said trying to change the subject.

"Seriously, Maebeth, is it still all good?"

"Oh, Lily, you can't believe how wonderful this visit has been." I went on to describe Luke's home, the beach and Miss Daisy.

"What's up with Slinky?"

"Lily, we've had a lovely few days and she'll fill you in when we get together this weekend."

When Slinky got back from Lucy's, I laid out my Get Lenny plan.

"Oh, my God, that's hysterical," she said. "Count me in." Next, I rang up Charo. She picked up on the first ring.

"Hey, sweet Charo. I'm coming home tomorrow, but Luke asked me to call and see if he could take you out to lunch Saturday. Just the two of you."

"Ya know, I might just seduce him, Maebeth."

"Don't mess with me, old woman."

The Meeting

The weekend was superb. I couldn't believe how much I missed my friends and Mr. Silverman. It had only been not quite a week but it seemed like a lifetime.

Luke had a long talk with Jack who arrived on Saturday.

Charo couldn't stop grinning since her date with Luke.

I was just glad to be out of the cowboy boots and other crap that I graciously returned to The Goddess.

Luke headed back to Malibu.

It was almost 3:00 p.m. and I started over to The Way of the Cross for our meeting.

We didn't do this often so there was some apprehension as everyone began to file in and take a seat.

I called the meeting to order—if "Let's Go" is correct parliamentary procedure.

Carmen immediately offered everyone iced tea and Hermit Flax Cookies, which she had baked that morning.

I shot her a glare. This was disruptive.

Everyone jumped up and grabbed a cookie and a glass of iced tea and sat back down.

So did I.

"Okay, any other announcements from anyone so we can get this show started?" I asked.

It was quiet.

As planned, I said Slinky had some news she wanted to share with us.

You could hear a pin drop.

"Oh my dear, dear friends," Slinky said. "There was a reason for my somewhat reclusive behavior this past week. I learned that I have advanced colon cancer."

Gasps.

"Oh, no," Julie said.

"Fuck," Honey said.

"My sweet child," Charo said.

"Lawdy, Lawdy, Lawdy," Lily said.

"Can I get you something?" Carmen said.

"Let her continue," The Goddess said.

Slinky spoke of her cancer and her plans. She told everyone about her wonderful trip to Malibu and how blessed she was to meet Lucy Bergmann. She also filled everyone in on Miss Daisy and Luke's beautiful home. She was upbeat yet relaxed and I could feel her magnetic energy permeate the room.

Slowly, Charo stood and walked over and embraced her. Then everyone else circled her—The Goddess, Carmen, Julie, Lily and Honey.

Slinky was moved and I could see her struggling to maintain her composure.

"You are such a wonderful family," Slinky said.

"Alright, I know this is a lot to comprehend, but we are sisters and as such I know Slinky can count on all of us, anytime, anywhere," I said.

Tissues were out, eyes were dabbed and lots of nods.

"Okay, now there is a remaining piece of business that I want to get your thoughts on." Today's tee read *NO BS*. I had chosen it carefully for this meeting.

"We all know that roadkill Lenny has been bothering our Honey. That creep is a menace and danger to all of us," I said.

I felt I was in a Baptist church as the "oh, yeahs," "he be one bad dude" and "castrate the bastard" rang out.

"We all know that my Luke has done his best to scare this little prick, but it's not working. I have an idea, but before I lay it out for you, I'd like to show you a clip from a movie."

Next I turned on the TV and pushed the DVD button.

Michael Madsen's Mr. Blonde filled the screen as he did his dance around the cop he was terrorizing with a straight razor.

Some of the ladies had seen *Reservoir Dogs* before, some hadn't and they were riveted.

After the cop's ear came off, I turned off the TV.

More gasps.

"Maebeth, have you lost your mind?" Carmen said.

"Man, that's one violent cat," Lily said.

"I could throw up," Julie said while getting out of her chair to let Sue in.

The Goddess added that it made her sick, too.

"What's the point of all this, Maebeth?" a somewhat stricken Honey said.

"I think we're going to torture the little rat bastard," Charo said.

"Bingo!" I said.

Showtime

I laid out my plan and got more suggestions from the group.

Basically, Honey was going to lure Lenny to Heave where we would tie him up and "torture" him with all the things we could come up with that would make a flaming misogynist nuts. We had no plans to hurt the little SOB physically, but wanted to teach him a lesson about messing with any of us.

We had a couple of things we needed to do to set up The Way of the Cross. Lily was in charge of the room renovations.

The Goddess was going to handle costuming and props, while our chanteuse team of Julie and Honey would provide the music.

Slinky and I had hatched the plan so we were going to be the administrators.

Charo and Carmen would handle the food.

Everyone would be the "entertainment."

We estimated that it would take a day to set up. On Monday, Honey could throw out the lure requesting a Tuesday morning rendezvous and getting his hairy butt over to The Way of the Cross.

Hopefully we would have the little prick crying for mercy in two days, or less, if we were lucky.

Everyone swore to total confidentiality. The only "outsider" was Jack who was staying with Slinky and she assured us that he would probably crack up laughing at the whole thing.

The meeting broke up and Slinky and I held hands. We had gotten through what could have been very difficult by sidetracking with our plan for Lenny.

"God does watch out for us, Maebeth," Slinky said.

When Monday rolled around, I rolled out of bed early and eager to resume my routine with a run to The Crossings. Mr. Silverman had been so thrilled to see me that he opted to spend the night in my bed and leave his normal nocturnal pursuits for another time.

I kissed him between his sweet ears and headed for the road. I had returned all my seductress clothes to The Goddess and was back in gray sweats and a tank top that read *Beat Bobby Flay!*

Everyone at the general store was glad to see me and said they had started to worry during my absence. Today I purchased an energy bar along with a bottle of water. I was going to need all my strength to pull this off.

You're toast Lenny!

Tough Love

This was L-Day. Our boy was on his way over to Honey's. Slinky and I ran a last minute check with the Heave team. Everything was in place.

"I think we're set. Let's roll," I said.

At 10:00 a.m. we took our positions in The Way of the Cross.

Honey was walking Lenny over under the pretense that she had something she wanted to give him. The greedy little bastard followed her right into our hands. Like a lamb to slaughter.

The minute he walked through the door, Honey kicked him in the butt and he went flying facedown.

"How's that skinny little ass feel now?" Honey said.

The Goddess and Lily pounced on top of him and got his hands behind his back.

"I've got a pretty bracelet for you, creep," The Goddess said. She had her own pair of handcuffs (we didn't ask) and snapped them on the little weasel.

"Mother fucker," Lenny said.

"Shut your face," Honey said.

"You're dead, bitch," Lenny said.

Honey started to whistle "If I Had a Hammer."

Julie and Carmen helped drag Lenny over to a straight back chair and plopped him on it.

"Sit up straight," Carmen said. "Where are your manners?"

Slinky and I were on our knees wrapping duct tape around his ankles.

"Nice ankles," Slinky said. "Bet the boys in the pen thought you were a real cutie."

Everyone was getting into it.

Charo slapped a piece of tape across his mouth and said, "Here you go, cockroach."

The little shit's eyes were bugging out of his head.

Honey kept whistling and everyone was breathing hard from the activity.

I calmly walked back and forth and introduced each one of us at length.

"Listen up, douche bag. We plan to spend some quality time with you. Maybe it's days, hours, maybe it's forever. You'll be here as long as it takes for you to mend your ways."

I cuffed him lightly under the chin.

Lenny was red-faced and gurgling now.

"Save it, shithead," I said. "How about some TV? See we aren't all that bad. Why don't you gather your thoughts. We'll be back in a while."

I wheeled the TV over.

"Honey, you know this faggot better than any of us. Which channel do you think he'd enjoy?" Slinky said.

"Hmmm, I bet Lifetime would be fun for my little sweetcakes," Honey said.

During our planning we figured that a couple hours of Lifetime would be enough to drive anyone insane.

Three hours of TV broken relationship dramas later, Carmen returned with a green salad with tiny finger sandwiches. She ripped off the duct tape over his mouth and told him she'd be happy to feed him since he would be needing his strength.

"Go fuck yourself," Lenny said.

"Oh, if only I could," Carmen said.

Carmen stuck the tape back over his mouth, put the salad on one of the two card tables that had been set up in the room, and changed the channel to Shopping Network before leaving.

After a few hours of that, Honey returned with Julie who was renowned for being able to weep at even supermarket openings.

They turned the TV off and started to talk about Slinky's situation. Both started to sob while Lenny looked ready to explode.

Tears streaming down her face, Honey removed the duct tape from Lenny's mouth and asked if she could feed him some salad.

"Drop dead, bitch, I'll see you in hell first," Lenny said.

"Oh my, Julie," Honey said. "I think sweetums is mad."

"No TV now, Lenny," Julie said. "You've been a bad, bad boy."

We reconvened out by the pool for our next move. We figured Lenny would be getting pretty hungry by now.

Charo went in first carrying a pan of fried chicken. Lily followed with mashed potatoes, gravy and sweet corn. Julie had a big chocolate cake while The Goddess hauled in in two 6-packs of Bud.

We moved Lenny's salad and finger sandwiches onto the floor, shoved the two card tables together, popped open a few Buds, clinked cans and started to eat.

"I just love these tatters all gravied up, mmm mmm," Lily said.

"But they're so much better when you can wash them down with a cold beer," Julie said.

"How's that fried chicken?" Charo asked.

"It's better than sex," Honey said. "Of course what wouldn't be after what I've been used to. Ain't that right, el pollo loco?"

We all roared and kept eating as nosily as we could.

"Honey, are you saying little love muffin here is a little short in the love department?" I asked.

"Maebeth, that ain't the only place that boy is short," Honey replied.

139

"Anyone for another brew?" The Goddess said.

"Hell yes," Charo said.

"Oh Lenny, please excuse our manners, it's been a long day and you, poor boy, haven't had a thing to drink or eat. We sure wouldn't want you to get dehydrated," Slinky said going over and removing the tape over his mouth.

This time Lenny shut up.

"Can we get you something to eat?" Slinky asked.

I licked the chicken grease off my finger and opened a can of warm Diet Coke.

"Here baby, I put a straw in it so it's easier for you," I said.

Lenny glared at me but sipped at the Coke. It must not have been too refreshing because he spit it out all over me or maybe he was just being funny.

"Never piss off an Italian," Carmen said as she came over and handed me a napkin.

"Just to show you how nice and forgiving I am, I'm going to leave the duct tape off your mouth, but the moment you make a sound, it's back on," I said.

"Okay girls, let's play some cards," Julie said as we all helped to clear the dishes and set up the card game.

We played for another two hours making as much small talk as we could. We droned on and on and Lenny looked as if he was going to snap.

At about 9:00 p.m. we turned the lights low and said we had a surprise for our boy.

Slinky went over to the DVD player and popped in a porn tape.

Lenny looked like he had just stepped off the planet.

We all left and got ready for our next move.

About an hour later Lily came back into the room and turned up the lights. The pig Lenny had had a little accident in his pants. Sexy movies will do that to you.

"Well, Lenny honey, looks like you're havin' a good time after all," Lily said. "But we have a nightcap for you while you're all turned on."

At that point music to "The Stripper" blasted into the room and Charo entered wearing only a red lace thong, matching Wonderbra, black fishnet stockings fastened with garters around her thighs and tennis shoes.

She waltzed over to a pole that we had installed on Monday and began her dance.

We were watching from the outside windows and were all laughing so hard I thought we'd have accidents in our pants, too. We even allowed Jack to take a peek and he was convulsed with laughter, which absolutely delighted Slinky.

Just like Mr. Blonde, Charo danced around, in this case the pole, doing as many sexy moves as she could for someone pushing 90. Then she sashayed over to Lenny and thrust her Wonderbra into his face. Quickly she twirled around, bent over and gave him a good view of her fanny.

Back up, circling around him again and then straddling him and giving it all she had.

Lenny was gagging now.

"Let's put our hands together for Miss Charo Blake," I screamed as we all came back in the room. Charo took her bows to our applause.

"Oh, you meanies," Honey said with her hands on her hips. "Julie, please cut the leg tape so I can walk Lenny to the bathroom."

Lenny was strangely silent as he shuffled to the bathroom with Honey.

When they returned, we duct-taped his legs again only this time we placed him on a blanket on the floor. Honey gave him another sip of Diet Coke and fed him a couple finger sandwiches and some wilted lettuce, which he suddenly had a taste for.

In unison we shouted, "Lights on, sleep tight."

With that we exited and high-fived each other out by the pool. Charo was still taking deep bows and we told her to go home and put some clothes on.

Jack was stretched out on a chaise and couldn't stop shaking his head and mumbling stuff that started with "those girls."

The plan was for each of us with the exception of Charo to take an hour's watch out by the pool to make sure our boy didn't get away. It would be easy to see anything because the lights were shining bright in The Way of the Cross.

What a sorority this was. Or would "coven" be a better description?

Girls Just Want to Have Fun

Lights were still shining brightly at The Way of the Cross as I started my run the next morning. I was wearing one of my favorite tees. A faded navy cotton with white lettering which read *Bye Felicia*.

It had been a quiet night and Lenny hadn't moved from his blanket on the floor. Probably having erotic dreams about Charo.

Today's plan was that Charo and Carmen would whip up a huge breakfast that we would eat in front of Lenny. Between the aroma, smacking lips and our girl talk, he'd go a little crazy. But first we orchestrated some entertainment to wake the little weasel up. This would be good.

We wore bathing suits. There was a lot old flesh and sagging body parts, but none of us was embarrassed.

Honey and Julie had managed to get Lenny up and into the bathroom. Now he was freshly ducted and sitting back in his chair. The tape was off his mouth but he wasn't saying anything.

Honey turned on the boombox and we all marched in to heavy bass and Tom Jones singing "Do You Think I'm Sexy." Every one of us shook our stuff and lip-synced past Lenny. Then we launched into our version of high kicking, a big finale which had been choreographed by Slinky, our resident dance pro.

Coffee and orange juice were already set up and plates of eggs, bacon, hash browns, sliced tomatoes, sausages and muffins were on the table.

We all sat down, a little breathless and heaped hot food on our plates.

"Where are our manners?" said Honey, as she got up and grabbed Lenny's Diet Coke from last night. "Here, Lenny, you want to finish this?"

"Help, I surrender. Youse win. I wan' outta here. I'll do anythin' youse wan'. Promise, honest injun, I'll never come back. Oh, pleeeeease," Lenny cried.

"Are you sure? We have *Legally Blonde* already in the DVD player for you," Julie said.

"That's not all. We have the latest issues of *Vogue*, *Elle* and *Bazaar* here for you to peruse," Slinky added.

"Lenny, first you have to sign this agreement that you will never step foot on this property again, nor will you have any contact with anyone here, especially Honey Dean," I said as I walked toward him with pen and paper.

He nodded.

The Goddess uncuffed him as we all formed a circle around him in the event he decided to rabbit.

Ever the nurturer, Charo asked him if he wanted some food.

"Nah, I jus' wanna go home. I wan' my mama," Lenny wailed.

"Awwww lawdy, and here we thought you didn't like the ladies," Lily said.

We undid the duct tape around his legs and helped him out of the chair.

He was wobbly and Honey took his arm and steadied him as we all headed to the road in front of Heave.

He slowly got on his Harley, revved it up and took off. No thanks for the hospitality, no goodbyes and no I'll miss you's.

We stood waving at his sad little backside and then broke into a war dance.

Seemed as if everyone had been empowered. Carmen, who'd been reluctant at the start, had a crazed look about her.

Charo was flipping Lenny's back the bird.

Lily was patting Beau's head and telling him to go after that boy's ride and eat the tires if he ever saw him again.

Slinky and Julie had their arms linked and were doing their best imitation of Celtic cloggers.

The Goddess was Mae West all over again, one hand on her hip and the other twirling the handcuffs.

Honey was pacing back and forth in front of us looking every bit the judge, nodding her head and saying, "Oh, yeah, oh, yeah, oh, yeah."

I grinned.

You can put your money on the wisegals.

Call Me

Fall was approaching and the cool weather was welcomed with a bit longer and later morning run.

When I got back to Heave, I noticed a Frontier truck parked in front of Honey's. I figured either she'd met someone new or was having trouble with her phone.

I said hello to Lily who was having coffee on her front porch and headed in for a shower. Mr. Silverman was waiting for me at my front door and I opened the door for both of us.

After a long, hot shower I threw on a pair of jeans and a chambray shirt and headed over to Charo's to see if there was anything cooking.

And, of course, there was an egg white omelet with my name on it and I dug in and listened as Charo wanted to relive her brief stint as a pole dancer.

"Did ya think I was hot?" Charo said.

"Charo, to tell you the truth I was getting a little turned on," I said.

"I'm thinkin' I'm going to suit up for Lester," Charo said.

"How's his cardiac situation?" I asked.

"Maybe you're right. I wouldn't want to kill him.

Maybe I'll omit the pole dancing and just do the push-up bra, thong and fishnets."

I nodded.

Carmen came in the back door.

"What's with the Frontier truck? My phone's working fine," she said.

"Maybe Honey's having some problems," I said.

Julie and Sue were at the back door. Julie had just finished her laps and was wrapped in a yellow terry robe which matched the omelet Charo was about to offer her.

Next came The Goddess through the back door, which in itself was unusual in that breakfast was not high on her list. She poured herself a cup of black coffee and sat down at the kitchen table with the rest of us. Here eyes were twinkling.

"Okay, cough it up," I said.

"Who, me?" The Goddess said.

"Yep, you. You're the only one here not feeding her face, you've got the floor," I said.

"Well-l-l-l ladies," The Goddess drawled. "There's an entremanure in our midst."

"What are you talking about?" Julie said.

"Seems like Honey is having a second phone installed," The Goddess said.

"So, big deal, I know she wants to pick up some extra money. The singing gigs are getting fewer the older she gets," I said.

"What's she up to, phone sales?" Julie said.

"More like phone sex," The Goddess replied.

"Holy shit, I'm in," Charo said.

"Someone ought to bitch-slap that broad," Carmen said with her hands on her hips.

"Is the Frontier man gone?" I asked The Goddess.

"Just left," she replied.

"Let's go," I said, heading for the back door.

It was like a parade with Julie and Sue, Charo, Carmen and The Goddess marching behind me as we went straight for Honey's back door.

Lily heard the commotion and joined us.

"You're going to love this, Lily," Charo said.

I knocked on Honey's door and she greeted us in an aqua silk kimono.

"Oh, you've heard," Honey said. "I could really use some tips on how to do this. Any ideas?"

Just then the new phone rang and Honey froze.

"Oh, God, I'm not ready."

We all filed in and gathered around the phone. Honey finally picked it up and said "hello" in a raspy voice a couple octaves lower than usual. She pushed the speaker button.

"Is this Desiree?" the caller asked.

The Goddess muffled a laugh and the rest of us were transfixed.

"Why, yes, this is Desiree, what can I do for you?"

At this point Carmen had had enough and stormed out.

Lily had not yet been brought up to speed and stood there with her mouth open.

"You can tell me what you're wearing," the caller said.

"How about you tell me your name," Honey said.

"John Holmes," the caller said.

"Oh, brother," The Goddess whispered.

"That's a nice name," Honey said.

"I asked you what you're wearing," the caller said.

"Oh, this old thing?" Honey said.

The Goddess rolled her eyes and made a cutting stroke across her neck.

"So, John, do you have children?" Honey asked.

"What?"

"I wonder if you have a family and a nice house and a dog," Honey said.

"What the fuck is this?" the caller said. "I'm getting my money back. Jesus."

And he hung up.

Honey held the phone away from her ear and said, "Now that's just rude. Here I am trying to make a good impression."

"Oh boy, oh boy," The Goddess said as she pretended to bang her head against Honey's living room wall.

"Let me take the next call," Charo said. "But first I want to get into my pole dancing outfit so I can get into the mood."

"What we have here is a learning curve situation," The Goddess said. "I was planning on taking a sick day today. I'm getting a little tired of the stockbroker job so maybe I can do a little tutoring."

"Could someone please tell me what the blazes is goin' on? What am I missin' here?" Lily said.

"What a morning," I said. "I need to talk to Luke. Get some sanity back in my life."

"What the hell is goin' on in this hood?" Lily asked.

"Come on, neighbor, I'll fill you in," I said as we exited the back door.

The Business Plan

Luke got the hiccups from laughing so hard.

"Babe, you're killing me. What's Honey's number? I need to hear this for myself."

"I wouldn't tell you if I knew it," I said. "There are enough pervs around here as it is."

"Anyway, I don't think John Holmes will be calling Desiree again."

"John Holmes, is that the name he gave?"

"Yes, do you know him?"

"Maebeth, you are telling me you've never heard of John Holmes?"

"Nope, who is he?"

"Just an internationally known porn star, infamous for the length of his johnson."

"Now, tell me how a nice Italian Catholic girl would know that?"

"Babe, okay if I come out this weekend? I'd like to see this operation for myself."

"I'd be upset if you didn't. Anyway, The Goddess is going to teach Honey how to talk dirty and maybe I'll go over there and pick up a few pointers to spice up your visit."

"I'll leave early and drive fast. By the way, has Honey heard any more from Lenny?"

"I don't think so," I said with my fingers crossed.

Maybe I'd water the story down and tell him a little over the weekend.

I couldn't resist heading back over to Honey's and was walking in the door when her phone rang again.

"Hello, this is Desiree," Honey said.

I could tell this was a big improvement already.

The speaker phone was on. The Goddess was sitting on the sofa with a notebook and pen.

"Hello, Desiree. What a sexy name. Give me an idea of someone famous you look like," the caller said.

Honey looked confused and then blurted, "Katie Couric. I'm a dead ringer for Katie Couric."

The phone went dead.

"Honey, what are you thinking? Katie Couric isn't exactly beat-off material, if you will excuse the French," The Goddess said.

"Well I was glancing at the coffee table and Katie Couric is on the cover of the *TV Guide* so that's what I came up with."

"That was your best shot?" The Goddess asked.

"Pooh, this isn't as easy as I thought it would be," Honey said.

"Okay, maybe you need to be wearing something sexy so you can get more in the mood for this. Lying doesn't seem to be one of your strong points," The Goddess said.

"I'll go in the bedroom and put something else on," Honey said.

I was at Honey's back door when I saw Charo walking across the pool deck in her pole dancing outfit.

Jack and Slinky were reading the newspaper out by the pool and turned to stone as she waved and paraded by.

"Guys, I'll fill you in later," I said as I went into Honey's determined not to miss any of the action.

"Maebeth, Lenny's not back, is he?" Slinky said.

"Nope, it's way better than that. I won't be long."

Honey was sitting next to the silent phone looking like a sex kitten in the most ridiculous see-through pink baby dolls I'd ever seen.

Charo strutted over to a straight chair, did a few half-assed knee bends and plopped down on the La-Z-Boy recliner by the TV. This was not a pretty sight.

The Goddess was at the kitchen table making notes.

The phone rang and I impulsively grabbed it and winked at everyone. How hard could this be?

"Is this Desiree?" the caller asked.

"You bet it is, sugah. How you doin'?" I said.

"Hmmm," the caller said. "Are you creamy?"

"Actually, I'm more olive-skinned," I said. "I'm Italian and when I get out in the sun, I really take a tan. Of course, you have to be careful of skin cancer no matter what your skin tone. I always use a high SPF no matter what. For instance, I just bought some Clarins hand cream that's SPF 15. You can't be too careful. It was expensive but beats those nasty age spots. Probably should wear gloves when I'm driving, but you know how that goes. Who thinks to do that? So, to answer your question, no, I'm not creamy."

Dead silence.

"Hello, hello," I said. "I think we got disconnected."

The Goddess was now banging her head on the kitchen table.

"Hey, I'm new at this. Give me a break," I said.

"I liked that sugar part," Charo said. "I thought he was thinking cream and sugar."

"MAYBE HE THOUGHT HE WASN'T GETTING HIS MONEY'S WORTH," The Goddess screamed.

I had never seen her lose her cool. This was fun. Even angry she was gorgeous.

"I'm never going to make a go of this," Honey said on the verge of tears.

"Look, it's your first day. You have a lot to learn. We'll get through this," The Goddess said regaining her composure.

Carmen walked in and shrieked when she saw Charo and Honey.

The Goddess explained to her how we had bombed on our first three phone calls.

Carmen listened intently and nodded like she understood.

The phone rang again and Carmen moved like a gazelle to grab it. She put it on speaker.

"This is Desiree," she said in her regular voice.

"I've been such a bad boy," the caller said.

We all looked at each quizzically.

"Mama doesn't like bad boys", Carmen said in a very schoolmarm voice.

"I'm so sorry, I'll try to be good" the caller said. "It's just that I'm been so very, very bad."

"Maybe my bad boy needs to be punished," Carmen said.

"Oh, please don't hurt me even though I've been so very, very bad," the caller said, his breathing quickening.

"Maybe a little spanking is in order," Carmen said. "Take your pants down. Take them down now."

"Oh, I don't have any pants on because I thought you were going to punish me. Oh, oh-oooh."

The phone call was over.

Carmen hung up, clapped her hands together, stood up, saluted and headed for the door.

"I'll be out by the pool doing some gardening if any of you need any advice," she said.

We nodded in unison.

Free Spirits

Lily and I were sipping a brew on her porch as the Heave neon sign came on. It was my favorite time of the year, knowing another desert summer was behind us and we had cool mornings and evenings ahead.

We were chuckling about Honey's phone sex operation when The Goddess asked if she could join us. She had a short glass of straight tequila in her hand and remarked it had been an interesting day.

"Did anything happen after I left?" I asked.

"God, Maebeth, Charo took the next phone call and got all pissed when the guy said he liked teenagers. She launched into a tirade about what the hell was wrong with older women and hung up on him."

Lily started in with "Oh lawdy, lawdy."

I was a little concerned. The Goddess' behavior was off. She never missed work, never complained about work and didn't often spend evenings chatting it up with the girls.

True, she was the youngest and only one at Heave with a fulltime job and she did prefer spending her down time with the boys, which is exactly what Chris was.

"You seem a little strange. Anything going on that your older sisters might help you with?" I asked.

"Can't put anything past you, Maebeth. I think I need to make some changes in my life. I've been feeling like I'm in a rut for some months now.

Just seeing Honey trying something new has got my juices flowing. I'm a good businesswoman and I've got some ideas."

"Anything specific in mind?" I said.

Be a good time for a prop plane to fly by with M-E-N-O-P-A-U-S-E trailing behind it.

"Actually, I'm just enthralled with funerals," The Goddess said. "Not the old-fashioned kind but real celebrations. Parties with themes, quality catering, music, you know, a real send off. Plus, if there is a viewing, do you know anyone better than me who could do makeup and hair? But that would be different, too. Say I interview the family and find out that the deceased always wanted to surf. Okay, so she's 93-years-old, but I give her a current windswept hairdo that sets her up for her next adventure."

I nodded.

"Wow," Lily said. "That's cool."

"That's not all," The Goddess said warming to our enthusiasm. "Take epitaphs. It's a lost art. They once were so creative but now it's name, year born, year died and maybe something about angels or whatever. Maebeth, you're a writer, you could be in charge of the epitaph division. Just look how wonderful your t-shirt collection is. You'd be a natural."

"You might have a point," I said. "In fact I used to love to visit old cemeteries and read the epitaphs. Probably something left over from my favorite flick *Harold and Maude*. Anyway, I've had my epitaph picked out for years."

"Really!" The Goddess said. "What is it?"

"Oh, you might have heard it before," I said. "It's: *I told them I was sick.*"

"Touching," Lily said. "I kinda like what Gloria Allred's got picked out."

"And that would be?" I said.

"Under here, we're all equal."

"And then there's that whole thing about urns," The Goddess said. "Why do they have to be so ugly? Put the ashes in wind chimes, stuffed animals, glass ornaments, jewelry, paperweights."

Lily nodded.

"You've been doing some heavy thinking," I said.

"Hereafter, I'm all about the hereafter," The Goddess said.

"Catchy," I said.

I heard someone approaching.

"I'm hot, horny and wet," Honey said, as she joined us and pulled up a chair. She repeated her new mantra three times using different voices.

"That's a lot better," The Goddess said. "There's hope yet."

"I think I've got this phone sex business figured out, finally," Honey said.

"We're all ears," I said.

"Okay, listen to this. I've been a singer and around musicians all my life. It's what I do. So why shouldn't I mix in what I'm good at with what I'm still learning? I already tried it on the last caller and although he sounded a little confused at first, he didn't hang up. Remember the song from *Gypsy* that said 'you gotta have a gimmick'?"

"So what's your gimmick?" Lily asked.

"Let's hear it," The Goddess said.

"A whistling vulva," Honey said proudly.

Sing out, Louise.

First Customer

Slinky stopped by the next morning and over coffee I brought her up to date on Honey's business.

"Oh, that's hysterical, Maebeth."

It was good to see her laugh. I hadn't seen her much since Malibu. She had been spending a lot of time with Jack whom she told to go back to New York for a while and tend to his business. Jack was reluctant, but she said she had other things to get in order and knew it would be better for him if he stayed busy.

"I'm going to miss all this craziness."

"Oh, Slinky," I said.

"Come on now Maebeth, my mind is in good shape. I'm not feeling sick. And, did I tell you that Lucy is coming this weekend?"

I smiled.

"And my sister Mavis is flying in from Singapore the following weekend. Maebeth, I don't have time to feel sorry for myself. There's too much to do. And, I want to say my goodbyes while I'm still feeling okay. I do have a big favor to ask you, Maebeth."

"Anything, Slinky," I said choking back a sob.

"Would you look after Ms. Early? I know she comes to you when I'm not home and I'd like her to continue that."

"Of course. I have to be the only one in the world who has a cat that likes a bird. And I like her, too."

"I'm still up in the air about the funeral. I really don't want a big deal, but I know for some it's closure. Jack asked what my wishes were—whether or not I wanted to be cremated or buried. I told him to surprise me, but I know I'll need to make a decision on that."

I hesitated to tell her about The Goddess' possible new career, but I went ahead and told her a little.

Slinky sounded thrilled with the whole concept and couldn't wait to get with The Goddess.

"I don't think Jack will want much of what I have in my unit other than some personal mementos. After all, he has his own place in New York and it's gorgeous. That being said, I would like each of you to pick out what you would like to have. I already feel wonderful just knowing that a little bit from my days at Heave will be in each of your homes."

"Oh, Slinky, must we do this now?"

"Maebeth, I refuse to hide from what's going on and what needs to be done. There are not many dreams in my life that have gone unfulfilled and I need to keep moving forward."

Later that day, The Goddess, Honey, Julie and I were sitting out by the pool nursing our early evening cocktails.

"What a journey," Julie said. "How'd we get from worrying about missed periods to planning funerals?"

"Well, at the time it seemed real important," Honey said.

"Has Slinky spoken to you about her funeral?" I asked The Goddess.

"She did, and we're working on a few things. I think it's great how she is handling all this. She is such a trouper," The Goddess said.

I needed to get to bed early. Lucy was driving down with Luke and Miss Daisy for the weekend and I wanted to get an early start to clean up my place and get in some groceries.

Micha and Frank were also going to spend the weekend in Monistat 1, so we needed to get that looking good. None of us had seen them since the wedding.

Charo was already in a dither about food and Carmen felt some organized activities would be welcome. I could sense that mandatory Rummikub contests and maybe some synchronized swimming classes were on the horizon.

I knew what my planned activity was going to be and it didn't involve games or swimming. My relationship with Luke had morphed into something quite comfortable. Our bond was as strong as ever and although the passion was still full throttle, there wasn't the anxiety that had previously come with separation.

This was a great place to be. I could continue my life at Heave and still have the thrill and excitement that ignited whenever we got together. Even his phone calls still set my heart fluttering. The big question in my mind was that since everything changes, how long would the scenario play out?

Just as I was getting ready to go home, Slinky came out her back door and joined us.

"What are you plotting?" Slinky said.

"We were just discussing whether 'Feelings' was the right tune for Honey's vulva," The Goddess said, not missing a beat.

Slinky nearly missed the lawn chair she was trying to sit in, she was laughing so hard.

"How about 'Happy Days Are Here Again'?" Slinky said.

"I was thinking more along the lines of the 'Star Spangled Banner,'" Julie said, illustrating upward movements with her hands.

"With the exception of Luke, of course, I would think 'It's a Small World' might be more on the mark," I said.

"Desiree, you do realize we have a business here to run?" The Goddess said as she stood up, straightened her dress, and said good night.

Oh, Hello!

I dressed in my black tee with *Carpe Diem* on the chest in white and black sweat pants. I thought the outfit looked particularly slimming, and that was the look I was going for because Luke would be arriving this morning along with Lucy and Miss Daisy.

It was a beautiful day and I felt I could have run for 10 miles. On the way back from The Crossings I was so engrossed in my thoughts that I didn't hear the rustling on my right. Not until a large tail slapped my thigh did I look down to see the beautiful Miss Daisy running next to me. I slowed and dropped down to my knees taking this magnificent creature into my arms. She was all legs and kisses.

The Jaguar slowly pulled up next to us and there sat Lucy and Luke, all smiles.

"Hi Lucy, hi hot stuff," I said.

Lucy got out of the car and we hugged.

"I've got an idea," she said. "It's been a long drive and Luke could use some stretching, not to mention that it would be good for Miss Daisy. Why don't I head back to Heave with the car? Luke said it was a straight shot from here. I'll call Slinky on the cell and she can meet me outside. What do you say?"

"Sounds great to me," Luke said, getting out as Lucy scooted over. "However, I do feel like I've got a little too much competition here now what with Maebeth and her four-legged friend all kissyface."

"Come here, big boy," I said grabbing his hand with one hand and waving goodbye to Lucy with the other. "Miss Daisy said she'd share."

There we were making out on the side of the road. Good thing it was early and there weren't any cars whizzing by. I just couldn't get enough of this hunk.

We jogged back to The Crossings. When we got to the general store, I went in for some bottled water and a paper cup for Miss Daisy while Luke and his best friend waited outside.

We snuggled on the curb, the three of us. What a sweet little family unit. Of course, we still had to make room for Mr. Silverman, or was it Mr. Silverman who had to make room in his busy life for us?

When we got back to Heave, Luke's car was parked in front of Charo's. Proof again that our olfactory function might be the strongest sense of all.

Charo came out to plant a big one on Luke. She was using a cane.

"What happened, Charo?" I asked.

"Maebeth, Lester was over here last evening and I was showin' him a few of my new pole dance moves when my big toe got hooked in the fishnet stocking and sent me head over ass. I'm okay, just a little sore. And up until the fall, I really had Lester goin'."

"Pole dancing?" Luke said.

"Uhhh, Buttercup, there are a few things I need to fill you in on. Just didn't want to bother you with all our doings here at Heave," I said.

I might be losing some of my charm because Charo was pulling Luke into her kitchen and I didn't see a lot of resistance. Charo already had met Lucy who was out by the pool sipping an orange juice with Slinky. I decided to join the culinary team. Hopefully, I'd need my strength for the fun and games to come.

After spinach omelets, toast, orange juice and cantaloupe, we headed back to my place with Miss Daisy, who commandeered the couch the minute we walked in the door.

Luke went to correct her, but I shushed him.

"What would Cesar say?" he asked.

"He'd say that my priorities at the moment involve the bedroom, not the living room," I said.

"First, a hot breakfast and now a hot babe. Am I a lucky man, or what?"

We were fast asleep in each other's arms when Miss Daisy started to bark. I got up, threw on a terry robe and went to the front door. It was Carmen announcing that Micha and Frank had arrived an hour ago and everyone was out by the pool. She and Charo had prepared a lunch buffet and we were to join them.

Luke showered while I went to check on Mr. Silverman. Poor guy was curled up on the back steps. I let him in and he and Miss Daisy started to check each other out. I thought it best to let them work it out and went in to shower and get dressed.

Dressed in a pair of tight pressed jeans and a navy turtleneck, I joined my three favorite hearts in the living room. Luke was in my lounger watching a football game and Mr. Silverman and Miss Daisy were curled up together, fast asleep on the couch.

A Kodak moment I would never forget.

The Gang's All Here

Luke always seemed so comfortable in his skin. He was wearing a soft gray warm-up suit that matched his hair. For a big man, he moved like a dancer. There wasn't an ounce of fat on him and he was impeccably groomed. He was elegant and I was so proud to show him off to my friends.

Everyone who hadn't yet seen him this visit stood up to give him a hug. Charo who had seen him earlier, gave him another. Luke was definitely family.

"Who's that beautiful dog?" Lucy said.

Daisy bolted and ran to her side.

Sue's ears perked up and she jumped off the chaise she was sharing with Julie.

Moe, Chris and Lester were slapping Luke on the back. I overheard talk about the game that was on TV and wondered just how long they would be by the pool.

"Gentlemen, you might want to postpone the loungers until you've sampled this feast," Charo said.

Lily and Carmen were coming out of Carmen's carrying bowls of food. They were followed by Frank and Micha who were loaded down with breads and condiments.

"Hot damn, check out Micha," Julie said.

My jaw dropped when I saw the married Micha. She was sporting a mullet, tie-dyed sweatshirt with matching floods. It was something out of the '60s.

"Hey, Micha, what's with the retro look?" I asked.

Frank wasn't much better. He had on an olive green Nehru jacket and a strand of orange wooden beads around his neck. His baggy jeans stopped at a pair of leather sandals.

"Listen to this ladies, we've opened a new store," Micha said.

Now it was Moe's ears that perked up.

"Our shop's called Abbey Road," Frank said. "It's right on the beach in Venice."

"Sign me up, I loved the '60s," I said.

"Let's not go there," Carmen said. "I know too much."

I nodded.

"Care to elaborate, Carmen?" Luke said.

"Uhhh, tell us about your shop, Micha," I said.

"Well, it's got a lot of throwback hippie clothing, incense, candles, books. Can you dig it?" Micha said.

Frank and Luke were catching up while Micha held court relating the highpoints of marital bliss. I wanted to hurl, but I thought I should eat first.

Sue wasn't having any of it either. She had strolled to Julie's back steps, curled up with her butt to the pool crowd. Sue had been top dog around here for too long and didn't appreciate the intruder.

The spread was delicious. Carmen had made her famous redskin potato salad. Plates of roast beef, turkey breast and cheeses were complemented by sliced tomatoes, carrot sticks, deviled eggs, stuffed celery, pickles and olives. Carmen had purchased fresh bread and rolls that morning.

Iced tea, Samuel Adams Light and a selection of soft drinks were on a table next to The Way of the Cross.

On a separate table was a large carrot cake that Charo had made the day before. Beside the cake was a sheet of paper with the recipe written in Charo's hand. At the top, underlined four times were the words: For Luke.

Carrot Cake

2 cups flour

2 tsp baking powder

1½ tsp baking soda

1 tsp salt

1 tsp cinnamon

2 cups sugar

1½ cups oil

4 eggs, beaten

2 cups grated carrots

1 8-oz. can crushed pineapple, drained

½ cup chopped nuts

Sift together flour, baking powder, soda, salt and cinnamon. Add sugar, oil and eggs and mix well. Add carrots, drained pineapple and nuts. Pour into two greased, floured 9" cake pans or 13"x9" Pyrex dish. Bake at 350 degrees for 35 to 40 minutes or until toothpick inserted near center comes out clean.

Cream Cheese Frosting

½ cup butter or margarine

1 8-oz. package cream cheese

1 tsp vanilla

1 lb. confectioners sugar

Cream butter and cream cheese, add vanilla. Beat in sugar. If too thick, add a little milk to spreading consistency.

Luke gave Charo a big kiss and thanked her for the recipe.

"That Lester is one lucky man," Luke said.

With the exception of Sue, everyone was having a great time.

We made up a plate and delivered it to Honey who was tied up on the phone. Evidently, she had found her niche with the whistling.

The men had excused themselves and headed for The Way of the Cross to watch the rest of the game.

Lucy turned to me and said, "Maebeth, there's so much love in this place. If anything should ever happen to Mel, I would want to live here with you all."

It Begins

That evening Luke and I took Frank and Micha to a Thai restaurant in Palm Desert for dinner.

It had been a full day. The happy couple was going to spend the night in the desert and head back early in the morning.

Luke was going to wait and see when Lucy wanted to go back to Los Angeles. I was looking forward to spending the night with him. Miss Daisy was sleeping over at Slinky's with Lucy.

When we got back to Heave, there was a note on my door from Lucy. Slinky had been feeling dizzy and had fainted. Paramedics were called and had taken her to the hospital. Lucy was going to follow and had left the door open to Slinky's so we could get Miss Daisy.

It was 11:15 p.m. Luke retrieved Miss Daisy while I called the hospital. Finally, I reached Lucy who said that Slinky was doing fine and was going to be released that evening and that she would bring her home and get her to bed.

Lucy's calm and remarkable kindness brought tears to my eyes. Here was this woman who had lovingly inserted herself into Slinky's final days. And, it was obvious to me that Slinky felt more at peace with Lucy than with Jack or any of her friends at Heave.

There must be something compelling about sharing your last thoughts with someone who didn't know your history. Slinky evidently took comfort in confiding her deepest feelings to Lucy and Lucy was totally immersed in her new friend.

Miss Daisy bounded into the room and Luke wiped away my tears and took me in his arms as I brought him up to date.

We got into bed and held each other tightly until our breathing became as one. I don't know who dozed off first, but the next thing I remember was a bit of light peeking through the bedroom window and Miss Daisy curled up on the floor on Luke's side of the bed.

I went to let Mr. Silverman in. I let the Washington family sleep in. I tiptoed into the bathroom, showered and grabbed some underwear, a fresh tee and an old navy warm-up suit. Today's shirt read *I ate Johnny Marzetti!*

What I really wanted to do is collapse in Charo's arms, but I could see from Lester's old Cadillac in front of her unit that her arms were full and the lights were out.

Maybe what I really needed was to be alone on my run and to concentrate on just how precious each moment is.

The run cleared my head and instead of going into my unit when I got back, I went out to the pool and crashed on a chaise. Julie was the first to appear as she came out to do her laps. She looked shocked to see me sprawled out and alone.

"Are you okay, Maebeth? What's happened?"

I filled her in on Slinky's situation. She got very quiet and pulled up a chaise next to mine.

"Oh, Maebeth, you knew this time was coming," Julie said. "Take comfort in that we're all going to face this in our own way, but the constant is that we'll all be here together for Slinky and for each other."

I nodded and held her hand.

Sue came over and sat at my feet.

Here I was, the so-called leader of the pack and now I appeared to be the one least likely to handle this with any kind of grace.

I stroked Sue between her ears.

Suck it up, Maebeth. Or as the sheep rancher said to that sweet pig Babe, "That'll do, that'll do."

Friends Forever

Luke headed back to LA with Miss Daisy. Lucy, after checking in with Mel, had decided to stay for the week. Mavis, Slinky's sister, was to arrive on Sunday.

Luke would return over the weekend and he and Lucy would go back to LA together.

As always, Charo's advice had been to stay busy. She was cooking up a storm for Slinky and Lucy.

No one saw much of Honey. Evidently her business was going full throttle.

I settled into my old routine of running hard every morning, working freelance a little harder than usual and clearing my unit of a lot of accumulated crap. Moving here had forced me to downsize, but there had been a steady piling up of clothes, papers and expired food.

Plus, I needed to make some room. Luke's presence in my life necessitated sharing some drawer and closet space and being a little more creative in stocking my pantry. For instance, dog food was now a staple.

Jack Renkforth called me daily from New York. I think he felt hurt that Slinky preferred Lucy to his ministrations. I tried to explain the situation as best I could, but this was all new to me, too. Jack felt that he wasn't getting the whole story and depended on me to tell him the truth when it came to Slinky's deteriorating health.

I felt pulled in between because I knew Slinky was trying to spare him. She had her own way of coping and we had to follow her lead.

Lucy had put notes on everyone's back door saying that Slinky wanted us to come over early Monday evening for cocktails and hors d'ouevres. No one had seen much of her since the weekend trip to the hospital.

When Monday arrived, everyone was seated in Slinky's living room. It was a beautiful evening with the sky streaked with pink ribbons. It was unusual for any of us to have a get-together in our units. Mostly because of the size, but also because of the wonderful outdoor venue we had created by the pool.

Carmen was in charge of making sure everyone had the cocktail of their choice.

Lucy and Slinky were sitting next to each other on the couch and roaring along with everyone else as Honey whistled "Are You Havin' Any Fun" and regaled the crowd with some of her more unusual phone requests.

The Goddess and Julie sat cross-legged on the floor with Julie rubbing Sue's tummy. Sue appeared to be in a much better mood now that Miss Daisy had hit the road.

When everyone has settled in, Slinky began to speak.

"I know this all seems a bit strange, but then this is the first time and for sure the last I will ever do this. Dying isn't such a bad deal when you have so much love in your life. I have been blessed with a very unconventional married life that has worked for both Jack and me and an equally wonderful and unconventional home in my later life here at Heave. How lucky can an old kick dancer get? I've asked you all to come into my home so you can walk through it and select something that you might like to have to remember me by. I know that's something that is usually done after one expires, but I would get such pleasure knowing that some of my favorite things are now in your hands. I have accumulated some pretty fine jewelry that Lucy and I have laid out on the bed. Obviously, this isn't about value, it's about what you would like. I've already set aside some family heirlooms for Mavis so everything here is up for grabs, as they say. Please don't be shy and for heaven's sake don't be sad. I'm not, but after the weekend's incident I felt I should move forward. Lucy has been a godsend. Mavis will be spending next week with me and Jack's coming back after that. Is that too much company or what?" she said getting a bit out of breath.

"Well, hell's bells Slinky, ya can't take it with you," Charo said, causing everyone to exhale and relax. "I personally will put my name on the copperware that's hangin' in your kitchen. I've coveted that for ages and I know I need to speak up before Carmen gets her claws on it."

Slinky beamed and said, "I love you Charo. Okay, girls, get up and look around. Don't be shy. I can't wait to see what you all choose." Lucy patted her hand and we all slowly got to our feet.

Julie hotfooted it into the bedroom at breakneck speed. The woman loved jewelry and latched on to an apricot diamond the size of a walnut. The Goddess chose a soft grey cashmere shawl that had been a favorite of Slinky's. Lily picked out a chunky turquoise necklace, while Honey selected a trio of gold bangles. Carmen was content with an art deco pin, while I selected a framed poster of the Ziegfeld Follies girls that hung in Slinky's bedroom.

"Carmen, please pick something out for Micha," Slinky said.

"How about that waste basket?" Lily said.

"No, I think she'd enjoy that roll of paper towels," Julie said.

"Really, ladies, that shaggy bathroom throw rug is more Micha's style," The Goddess added.

"Oh, for God's sake," Slinky said. "I'll just choose something myself. And Maebeth, please grab that extra bag of bird seed on your way out."

To the very end she would be thinking about other souls.

Moving Forward

Slinky would live another three weeks. She and Mavis had a good visit and Jack came back to stay with her. Both Jack and Lucy were with her at the end.

Slinky had prepared us to celebrate her life and it seemed that all of us at Heave were resigned to let go and wish her well on her next journey.

The ceremony was simple. She had been cremated and Jack was going to scatter her ashes on his next trip through the Suez Canal, as Slinky had requested at the end.

I didn't see Ms. Early for a few days, but finally she appeared one morning at my back door. I went out to greet her and she flew onto my shoulder. I stroked the back of her neck and it was as if she was grieving, for although she had done that with Slinky, this was the first for the two of us.

Slinky's unit now belonged to the remaining residents and it would be our task to vote in the next Heave resident. Although no one wanted to address the situation, it had to be reckoned with so that upkeep of Heave could be ensured.

We met the week following Slinky's death to begin our discussions. We were sitting on the floor in Slinky's living room. Jack had seen to it that Slinky's remaining possessions were removed from the unit. In my heart it would always be Slinky's home because she was an original Heave resident and no one but she had lived there. Her home had been imprinted with all that was so very unique to this amazing woman. This would be difficult.

Charo spoke up first. Her daughter, Sarah, had been one of the original eight and when she passed away we had voted in Lily.

"I know this has never come up, but would any of us object to having a man take over Slinky's unit?"

"I sure wouldn't," The Goddess piped up.

"Do you have someone specific in mind?" Lily asked.

Charo nodded.

"Well, mind you, this is just for discussion, but I think my grandson Sam is wanting to make a change in his life. He's getting tired of New York and had such a great time when he was last out here. Plus, he knows Palm Springs can always use a five-star interior designer."

"Shouldn't we also be looking at our waiting list?" Julie said.

"Indeed, we should," I said. "However, we have never had a rule that said 'no men allowed.'"

"If we did you'd be SOL," Honey said.

"I beg your pardon, Desiree," I said.

"Well personally, I'd love to have Sam at Heave," Carmen said. "It would be great to have someone as talented as he is around here. Plus, he's young and that would be refreshing."

"Do we know if Sam is even interested, Charo?" I said.

"I haven't mentioned it to him because I wanted to see what you all thought," Charo said. "And hey, Sam is goin' to be 46 so he's no baby anymore, although he'll always be a kid to me."

"Young is good," The Goddess said.

"Well, we don't have any rules against men or youth, although I always assumed this would be a place for women,"

I said. "We're basically ruleless. So far if you can fog a mirror and we think you'd fit, you're in."

"I think there's something comforting about having all mature women here," Julie said. "I do admit though that Sam fits in."

"Let's go over the waiting list. This is such a major decision for all of us," The Goddess said.

"Okay, we have the retired school teacher, the lesbian vet, the motivational speaker, the former dental hygienist, the concierge, the nurse and the photographer," I said. "Who wants to go first?"

"Christ, this is like sorority rush," Honey said.

"My vote is for either Sam or the nurse," Charo said. "At my age, I need all the help I can get."

"I like Sam a lot, but dental hygiene is so important," Carmen said.

"I like Sam, too, but I'm just not convinced this is the best place for a young man," Julie said.

"Don't knock it until you try it," The Goddess said.

"I haven't met the concierge, but aren't they always pleasant?" Lily asked.

"Lily, I voted for you sight unseen and look what a mistake that was," I said with a wink.

Lily grinned.

"She's right," Carmen said. "Not about you, Lily, because we are so lucky to have you here, but we were lucky that it turned out so well. Maybe we have to narrow it down and invite the candidates over for interviews."

"Okay, let's sleep on this and have another meeting in the next few days. Who wants a beer?" I asked.

The Interviews

A few of the ladies were invited over for coffee and brief interviews. Every one of the original owners had personally known at least one of the interviewees. I was friends with the lesbian vet and thought the world of her.

Her name was Amanda Masters and her beloved partner of 27 years had died the previous year. The consensus of our group was that she would be a great addition and it wasn't a bad idea to have a vet on the premises with Sue, Beau, Mr. Silverman, Ms. Early and the visiting Miss Daisy sharing our homes.

Charo had contacted Sam and he was thrilled to be considered. We weighed how pleasant he was to have around and how much he had contributed to our lives when he was here.

We took a vote and Sam won, hands down. Julie was the only one who still had reservations, but she came around and agreed that Sam would be an interesting addition to the mix.

Heave would be a place for Sam to begin anew. His move-in date was a week before Halloween, which was some weeks away. We decided that we'd send him an invitation to our next event which was annually organized by The Goddess who would look for any excuse to wear a costume or nothing at all.

Her invitation was off the wall.

Save the Date or else!

Witches & Wizard Brew & Dinner

Lo! Ye of the Witches Coven of Heave. A full moon is risin' tonight and a howling message for you is in the wind. Beware, the date is drawing near to welcome our handsome new wizard, dust off the cobwebs, and rev up the broomsticks.

Bloody Mary's Reception

Faux Fancy Feast of Liver of Old Lovers Salad, Gizzard Goole with Frogtoes Stew or Spaghetti Guts & Eyeballs,

Dripping Desserts of Broken Sweethearts, Dried Hops and

Toadstool Roots

6:30 p.m., Halloween, Heave poolside

Dress wicked.

It would be interesting to see what costume Sam might select. I had a feeling it would be over the top. Sam already felt like the right choice.

The Goddess and Honey went out by the pool and were already planning wardrobe, entertainment and decorations. Lily and Beau were headed back home. Julie went home to check on Sue. Carmen and Charo were hugging and excited about having Sam around permanently.

I was tired and couldn't get Slinky out of my mind. It didn't seem quite right that everyone could so easily move forward. Change was in the air and I wondered where I might be in another year. Here at Heave, in Malibu, or God forbid, in poor health facing my mortality.

Settle down, Maebeth. Settle down and concentrate on the moment.

The Trip

"Buttercup, it's me. How are you?"

"I just perked up kinda all over," Luke said. "Babe, just your voice can do that to me."

"Okay, I've got a plan. Now be honest with me and if you don't like it, tell me. I've never been to New England to see the leaves change colors and was wondering if we might find ourselves a romantic little bed and breakfast and take a leisurely road trip."

"Are you proposing, Babe?"

"You wish."

"Okay, let's see if I have this right. My Maebeth, who views coming over to Malibu as an ocean crossing, wants to fly across the country and drive through New England and look at trees."

"You forgot the part about the big old antique bed with the cozy down comforter, the crackling fireplace, excellent brandy and nothing to do but make hot love when we're not looking at some leaves. You know, checking out leaves really doesn't take up too much time."

"Your mama, I'm calling my travel agent the minute I hang up so you won't have a chance to change your mind."

"That's what I like, a man who takes charge."

"By the way, Babe, might I ask what brought this on or should I just leave well enough alone."

"Luke, let's do things together, be together and see where it takes us. I never want to let you go and I'm tired of being so careful so I don't get a broken heart."

"Maebeth, the only thing that has a rat's ass chance of getting broken is that old New England bed."

Beam me up, Scotty, I have just made a commitment.

Changes

Things were getting back to normal at Heave. Everyone was excited about Sam's arrival. Sam had already given Carmen specific instructions on Behr paint colors for his walls. Carmen was never happier if she had a project and now she was dedicated to getting Sam's new home ready. He had already put in an order at a local furniture store and he and Carmen planned to shop for accessories together. The only things he was bringing west were his cookware, clothes and a few mementoes. This was turning over a new leaf for Sam who wanted to leave his New York City life behind for a more tranquil environment. He would soon find out that life at Heave was anything but peaceful.

I was pleasantly surprised by my newfound travel urge. Spending some concentrated time with Luke would give us both some insight into whether or not we could stand living together for any length of time.

It was a beautiful morning as I laced up my New Balance running shoes and headed down the road. Today's tee read *fuggedaboutit*.

When I got back, there was a message from Luke. The travel plans had been made and we would be leaving in two weeks. It would be autumn in Vermont for the two of us with side trips to the White Mountains of New Hampshire and the Berkshires of Massachusetts. I could hardly wait.

I grabbed my cell and punched in Luke's number.

When he picked up, I screamed, "Paisan, I'm so freakin' excited."

"Is this Carmella?"

"Knock it off. It just hit me that I have nothing to wear that will work on the East Coast. Maybe I'll go on the Internet and see what L.L. Bean has to offer."

"Maebeth, I wouldn't get too hung up on your wardrobe because you won't have anything on most of the time."

Life was good.

We said goodbye and as I walked into the kitchen, I saw The Goddess standing at my door.

"I didn't want to interrupt while you were on the phone," she said.

"No problemo, I was just talking to the world's sexiest man."

"Maebeth, I wanted you to be the first to know. I handed in my resignation yesterday at Merrill Lynch. This is going to be a big loss of income for me, but I've saved some money and have decided to follow my heart and get into the funeral business. I mean, here's a market that will never go dead, so to speak. And with all the Latinos and old people in the Coachella Valley, how can I miss? Palm Springs truly **is** 'God's waiting room.'"

"So you're going to have to learn to make some pretty big transformations what with gunshot wounds and wrinkles," I said.

"Everyone deserves a proper send-off," The Goddess said, stiffening up just like a proper funeral director.

I nodded.

"Hey, I'm just kidding, I think it's a terrific idea and I'm proud of you for making this change."

"Well, I have already lined up to assist at a local funeral home. Lots of the Latino families want 24-hour wakes, so they can use some extra help. Plus, we're going to be offering in-home service and culturally themed programs. They used to ship bodies back to Mexico, but not so much anymore. I'll be hiring mariachis and brushing up on death customs."

"Do you speak Spanish?"

"Nada," The Goddess said.

Fall Is Here

Now that hot desert heat was a memory, nights and mornings were magnificent and all of us left our back screen doors open to take advantage of the fresh air. Our pocket books also appreciated not having the exorbitant air-conditioning bills that came with the territory.

Carmen was buzzing around with her fall flower project. She was planting bright red geraniums in hanging baskets poolside and in flowerbeds around the interior next to our back doors. I couldn't help but notice that Sam's unit seemed to be blessed with the most blooms.

The Goddess was looking for dark skin to practice makeup application. Lily apparently was too black so she went after the olive-skinned Italians, Carmen and myself. Currently she was working on me as I sat nervously on a kitchen chair and her endless bottles, jars and tiny sponges were scattered all over the kitchen table.

Luke was coming in for the weekend and would be here anytime so I was eager to get this over with.

"Sit still, Maebeth, I'm trying to get the upper eye liner just perfect. Remember, you're dead, your eyes will be closed so we don't have to worry about lower lid liner. The shadow is going to be so important. Can you please stop twitching."

"Hey, Goddess girl, this damn pancake makeup is so thick I can hardly talk."

"Oh, pahleeees, you won't be doing any talking. Can't you remember, you're deceased?"

"Girlfriend, I wouldn't be caught dead looking like this."

"I'd kiss you hello but you're scaring me," said Luke, who had quietly come through my front door, into the kitchen and was wearing a big grin.

"Oh, shit, now see what you've done?" I said.

"Hi, Luke," said The Goddess. "What do you think? I'm practicing my festive dead Latino look?"

"El pollo loco," said Luke. "By the way, that's the extent of my Spanish."

I tried to smile.

Luke grinned.

The Goddess sighed.

"Okay, I'm packing this up. Maybe Carmen will be more receptive. Hmmm, Luke, I could use some practice on a man. Are you willing?" The Goddess said.

"You bet, as long as you can match me up with Ms. No Expression. We need to look good together."

I got up from the table, held my arms straight out in front of me and munster-walked into the bathroom.

Mother of Pearl, I needed to get my ass out of here and to New England, pronto!

Good Morning

The plan was that Luke would spend the weekend at Heave and we would drive back to Malibu and veg out for a few days before we caught our plane out of LAX for Boston Logan International Airport. We were to have dinner our first evening with Slinky's Jack, who would be in town on business.

Luke was still sleeping Saturday morning when I woke and threw some clothes on for a run. I decided to do a few yoga positions out by the pool for a warm up. Years ago I had been a Bikram devotee, but the hot rooms finally got to me and I gave it up with the exception of a few favorite poses.

I was in the downward dog position when I spotted two furry, hot pink high-heeled slippers about five feet away from me.

It was Honey in a matching chiffon robe with fur trim that covered her see-through baby dolls. A Bluetooth was nestled in her right ear. She was working.

"For chrissake, Honey, Luke's inside and if he sees you he's apt to have a heart attack."

"I saw you out here and thought you could use some company. Hang on," Honey said, stretching out on a chaise.

"Honey, do I want to hear this?"

"Hello, this is Desiree, what can I do for you, sugar?"

"Please God, don't let her whistle," I said.

"'Lady of Spain,' you bet, I know it. Just a second toots, I need to put the phone down you know where," Honey said with a wink.

As she started to whistle, Sue meandered over with her ears back. Beau was at his back door and let out a howl. Sue plopped down and put her front paws over her ears. Beau wailed on. Luke came out with a mug of hot coffee and a shit-eating grin.

The Vulva Queen was whistling away as Charo's door slammed and she beelined for Luke.

I walked over to Luke and said, "This could be a while. Did you know a pig's orgasm lasts 30 minutes? I am outta here."

Luke, with his arm around Charo, said, "I'd join you Babe, but between Charo's offer of breakfast and the entertainment, I'm kind of occupied at the moment. And besides, your tee is making me nervous."

Today's message was *Honk if you're continent.*

Death Knocks

At first I thought we had left the TV on. I glanced at the clock on the nightstand and it was 5:15 a.m. It was Sunday and someone was wailing.

Luke woke up too and asked me if I had heard something. Both of us bolted from the bed and I unlocked the front door to find Lily sitting on the steps rocking back and forth and sobbing uncontrollably.

I ran to her, got down on my haunches and put my arms around her.

"NO, NO, NO," she screamed as she punctuated each word by slamming her fist against the cement stoop.

"Oh, God, Lily, what is it? Please, let me help you," I said.

Luke sat down next to Lily and drew her close to him. We managed to hear her say "My sweet Henry, my sweet Henry" over and over again.

We were soon to learn that her eldest son, Henry, and his girlfriend Ruth, had been killed the night before in an auto accident in Savannah. They had been returning from a church social when they were broadsided by a car full of drunken teenagers. None of the kids were killed, but two were seriously injured. Ruth had died at the scene and Henry a few hours later at the hospital. Dennis, Ruth's other son, had called his mother early Sunday morning. Benny, Lily's husband, had died a few years ago and never had been much of a father to his sons. Lily was everything to her boys and they were everything to her.

Maybe that was why neither boy had married. Lily had done a great job with her children and both were college graduates. Henry and Ruth had a six-year-old son named Nathan, who had been staying with Dennis while his parents were out. Dennis was openly gay and in a long-term relationship.

I stayed with Lily while Luke walked away to make a few phone calls. Charo and Carmen had heard the commotion and joined us. Only Charo had experienced the pain of losing a child and she suddenly looked her age as she tried to comfort Lily, getting her to her feet and walking her toward her porch glider. It was the oddest, most timeless tableau. This tall, regal black woman leaning against our old, short and wise Charo.

As Carmen and Lily sat on the glider while Charo made coffee, Luke came toward us. He squatted down at Lily's feet, took her long, thin hands in his, and said, "Lily, I've just gotten off the phone with the Savannah Police Department and with Dennis. Neither Henry nor Ruth suffered, it all happened so fast. Henry never regained consciousness. Funeral services are scheduled for Wednesday. Maebeth and I were heading east anyway next week and we will both accompany you to Savannah. I have made all of the arrangements. We will leave tomorrow for LA, grab a few things and fly to Savannah. We want to be with you. I hope I haven't been too forward."

If I ever doubted my love for this man, it would never be again. Lily was my friend, but Luke was doing this not so much for me, but for another human being—one he had the utmost respect for.

"How can I ever thank the two of you," Lily said. "I don't think I can get through this alone."

"Dear Lily, you are family and you will never be alone at Heave," said Charo as she walked through the door carrying a tray of steaming mugs of coffee.

By now, Honey, The Goddess and Julie had gotten the news and joined us on the porch. They were like sentinels closing in to protect one of their own.

The wake had begun.

Saying Goodbye

All the way to LA, Lily told stories about Henry and what a joy he had been. She was sitting in the front seat with Luke while I listened intently from the back.

Both of her sons were pharmacists.

"I guess it was a form of rebellion when I told those boys 'no drugs,'" Lily said.

It was the first time since receiving the news that she sounded like her old self.

She had spoken yesterday afternoon to Nathan and was certain he didn't quite understand all that was going on. She didn't want him to attend the funeral because she didn't want that to be the last memory of his parents.

While Luke had been busy yesterday changing our travel plans, I had hastily put together my Savannah/New England wardrobe. I hadn't planned on a funeral.

The Goddess was more preoccupied than usual.

Julie helped Lily with her packing and there wasn't a dry eye at Heave when we left for LA.

The late afternoon flight was uneventful with the three of us dozing off after an exhausting last 24-plus hours of emotions. First class seats weren't wasted as we toasted Henry's memory, clinking our flutes of champagne.

It was late when we arrived and Dennis met his mother at the airport. We would be staying at a local Westin while Lily bunked in with Dennis, his partner Izzy, and Nathan.

After a fitful night's sleep, we arranged to meet Lily's friends and family at the funeral home. Ruth's family was gathered in an adjoining suite.

Both caskets were closed and there was such an abundance of floral arrangements that many had to be directly diverted to a local hospital.

As always when the young die, there was a feeling of disbelief throughout the evening as visitors went from room to room, embraced, shared memories and offered their condolences.

We met Nathan who was allowed to witness the outpouring of love for a short time. He was a handsome young boy, already tall for his age and with dark brown eyes that danced when he talked.

Dennis could have been a professional linebacker. He was huge and solid, but all that muscle seemed deflated as he grieved openly, with Izzy never far from his side.

Lily took charge as she had so often had to do in the past. Tomorrow's funeral would be hard. Tomorrow would be the last goodbye.

The Funeral

Don't ask me how she did it, but The Goddess' touch was everywhere at the funeral. Unbeknown to Lily, Luke and me, she had been in contact with Dennis who in turn had cleared the funeral plans with Ruth's family. The Goddess had flown out early Monday morning and set up command central.

The funeral was to be held at the First African Baptist Church on Montgomery Street. I wondered if this historic landmark was prepared for The Goddess' magic wand.

Loose bouquets of sunflowers and daisies were tied at the end of the aisle pews. An enlarged picture of Ruth, Henry and Nathan hamming it up at someone's birthday party was on an easel between the two coffins. Each had puffed out cheeks like they had hamburgers in them, large glasses with big rubber noses and bushy eyebrows attached.

The Goddess had done her homework. This was to be a celebration. This would be a time for friends and the community to experience grieving, hope and joy. This would be a time to dance before the Lord.

Dennis gave a eulogy. He was eloquent in his admiration of this loving couple. He praised Lily and Ruth's parents for setting such a fine example for their children. He said that there would be long and loving arms encircling Nathan for the rest of his life. And then he said, "Hold it."

There wasn't a sound in the church.

Lily put her hands to her mouth.

"What if the tables were turned and Henry was up here yammering about me. You know what I'd think he'd point out. He'd mention once again that I have a wide ass. He'd recall the time I put a lizard in dad's lunch box. He'd mention just how horrified he was when he discovered a *Playboy* under my mattress. Of course, he'd neglect to say that I found it under his pillow. Henry was the kind of older brother one could only hope for. He always knew I wasn't quite like the other guys, which made him protect me even more. Henry had my back. He made my life and the lives of many of you here, fun and loving. I'm sure he's putting the moves on those up above to make sure I have a safe landing when I'm called up. Okay Henry, that's it for now, bro." With that, the choir launched into "Hit the Road Jack" and everyone started clapping. Iggy, who was about half the size of his partner, joined Dennis on the altar and they started dancing. The entire church poured out into the aisles and joined in the festivities.

Lily was shaking her head and chuckling, while shouting, "Lawdy, I'm goin' to whup that little shit." Luke grabbed both her hands, pulled up her and they danced with abandon.

The Goddess had maneuvered up the aisle and grabbed my arm. "I need help," she said.

I followed her to the back of the church where she handed me a stack of black cardboard top hats and a box of fans.

"These are our favors. Top hats for the gentlemen and fans for the ladies. We are in the south, if you recall."

"Oh, brother," I said. "Is this fucking Mardi Gras or a funeral?"

"Look, Maebeth, we are celebrating Henry and Ruth. This isn't yo mama's send-off."

I nodded.

True, everyone was having a marvelous time. First, out came the coffins and then a band of merry men and women donning coal-black top hats and colorful fans to ward off the stillness of the air. The wind had taken a nap and we were fanning away all cares for but a brief moment.

After solemn services at the cemetery, family and guests were invited to the church rectory parking lot where The Goddess' interpretation of finger food was overflowing sandwiches of pulled pork and roast beef. The barbecue also featured Angus beef hamburgers with grilled onions, hot dogs, salads, pies and a vodka-laced peach punch, not that anyone was pointing out the kick it had to the good reverend.

Little Nathan had joined the festivities and sat between Lily and Dennis.

"I think you've found your groove," I said to The Goddess, who was directing the caterers to replenish the punch.

"I don't want to say this has been fun, but it has been so rewarding. Damn, I know now I can do this. And the best part is helping out Lily and her family."

As if on cue, Lily walked up and reached her long arms around both of us. "What can I ever do or say that will thank you two wonderful friends? Your love and strength have gotten us through this."

"Oh, Lily, you would be there for us and you know there isn't anything your family at Heave wouldn't do for you," I said.

"Maebeth, I hope you and Luke can continue on and have your vacation," Lily said.

"Yes, we're leaving this afternoon for Boston where we are having dinner with Jack Renkforth. Then lord knows what Luke has planned. Are you sure there isn't anything we could still help you with here?"

"No, now comes the hard part. The reality of our lives without our Henry and his lovely Ruth. Ruth's parents are relieved that Dennis and Izzy have taken it upon themselves to sort through Henry and Ruth's personal things and work with the attorney. Because they were both so young, I'm not sure how much they had prepared for such a tragedy. As for Nathan, everyone has agreed that he will return to Heave with me and stay until we can figure out what's best."

That was all The Goddess needed to hear. She darted for Nathan and began to regale him about the upcoming Halloween party. I could see the young man was enchanted. Who knows if it was the content of The Goddess' conversation or The Goddess herself that momentarily took this young man's attention away from his loss.

"That girl is somethin', isn't she?" said Lily.

"She got attitude, grandma," Nathan said.

Lily grinned.

"Oh Christ, Lily, what's Nathan going to think when he sees Chris in that damn two-piece?"

"I think I'm going to have to watch carefully that all of you don't spoil him rotten," Lily said.

"Well, there's Charo's cooking, and Sam will welcome another fellow. And, did I mention, a swimming pool, Beau, Sue, Mr. Silverman and Ms. Early?" I said giving Lily a squeeze.

We've got your back, little Nathan.

Boston

When we arrived at the restaurant, Jack was already seated and nursing a Glenlivet. There were big bear hugs all around. Jack looked much better than the last time we saw him. He had immersed himself in his business and his global trips had left him little time for self-pity.

When the waiter approached, I ordered a pinot grigio and Luke pointed to Jack's scotch and said, "I'll have what he's having."

"So what's up at Heave?" Jack asked.

"Well, you know you are welcome to use Monistat 1 whenever you wish," I said.

Then I filled Jack in on Lily's tragedy, Sam's arrival and Honey's new phone sex venture.

"Jack, if you ever want to totally forget about sex, give Honey a call," Luke said.

Jack smiled.

"And you would be basing that on previous comparisons in your Frontier experiences, Mr. Washington?"

"Babe, I'm just saying that Honey, or should I say Desiree, should be thinking about a career switch."

"Oh, boy, I hate to put a halt to this discussion," Jack said as the waiter approached to take our order.

While the boys ordered Striped Sea Bass and Soft Shell Crabs, I opted for Roast Organic Amish Raised Chicken Under a Brick.

"Babe, I'm not even going to touch that," Luke said peering up over the large menu.

It was a wonderful evening and most welcome after the heartbreak of the past few days.

After the goodbyes we headed back to our hotel for a good night's sleep before the much anticipated fall road trip.

It's the most wonderful time of the year.

Falling Leaves

"**B**abe, aren't you curious where we're headed?"

"Buttercup, my G-P-S is O-F-F," I said, spelling the words out slowly.

"You're not getting squirrelly on me, are you?"

"Actually, road trips bring out another fascinating side of me that you're about to experience."

"Whoa, this should be good."

We were on a two-lane road heading north into New Hampshire. Already the leaves were a blanket of reds, oranges and yellows.

"Jump in anytime you want," I said as I started to belt out "100 Bottles of Beer on the Wall."

I was at 85 bottles and going strong when Luke grabbed my wrist and asked me if I had trained at Guantanamo.

"Jeez, what a spoilsport. Okay, I've got the perfect game. It's called 'Pig.'"

"Babe, you would not be so insensitive as to be referring to my former work in law enforcement?"

"Oh, you devil, you know I'm not. Here's how it goes. You say a letter of the alphabet, then I say a letter and the object of the game is to make a word that is at least five letters long and does not end on you. If it does, then you are a "p" and if you have two more words end on you, you lose—you're a p-i-g."

"Ladies first," Luke said.

"Okey-dokey, 'L,'" I said while twirling one of my ruby earrings around and tucking my feet under me.

Luke looked serious and then I caught a slight smile. "Hmmm, 'L,'" Luke said.

"I just said 'L,'" I said.

"So did I," Luke said.

I stuck my right thumb in my chest thinking "a" and pointed my right index finger at Luke and silently mouthed "m" and then it was the hooked thumb back into my chest.

"Fucking llama," I said. "You are such an asshole."

"Whoa, again, where's the love, where's the atta boy?"

I sulked.

I started to hum the Bee Gees' classic "How Deep is Your Love" and we both broke up.

"Okay, new game, we each have to tell something about ourselves that the other doesn't know. Let's call it 'Deep Dark Secrets,'" I said.

"This could get out of control," Luke said. "Are you sure you want to do this?"

"Yep, and this time you go first."

Luke was quiet for the longest time and then he began.

"Years ago there was a baby girl dropped off on the doorstep at a precinct where I did some work. She was shoved into a dirty paper bag and it broke your heart. She was only days old and no one came forward to claim her so a bunch of the cops made a pact that she would always have a handsome place to put her head down no matter how old she was. We called it 'The Eternal Guest Room Project.' A wonderful couple adopted the little girl and named her Molly. When she was old enough to understand, her parents told her about the project and how she had seven bedrooms in addition to her own that were waiting for her at any time. Molly corresponds with all of us from time to time.

She's married now with a family of her own. She's never really used any of our guest rooms, but has pictures of each on her mantel. So, if you've ever wondered how my décor veered off to girly, now you know."

Men are from Mars, because this sweet man has to be from another planet.

Room at the Inn

It was late afternoon when we arrived at The Sugar Lake Inn, which is located in the heart of the Lakes and White Mountain region. It was a restored Victorian farmhouse and looked charming with its wraparound porch, green shutters and large red barn.

Luke told me that there were only eight rooms and that the movie *On Golden Pond* had been filmed nearby.

"Okay, so who do you think I most look like, Jane or Katherine?" I asked.

"How about Henry?" Luke said.

I jabbed his arm.

Luke got the keys to our room which was named the Loon Room.

"Isn't that the name of a crazy bird?" I said.

"I think that's 'coot.'"

"Better not be 'coon,'" I said.

"Better watch your mouth," Luke said.

The room turned out to be warm and cozy. We dropped our luggage off and decided to stretch our legs and check out the quaint village.

I thought I was in a Norman Rockwell world. What was touristy was dwarfed by the surrounding natural beauty of the mountains, lakes and foliage.

I purchased a stack of postcards for the ladies back at Heave and we signed up for a Golden Pond Boat Tour.

After a day of wandering through folksy shops and a terrific lobster dinner, we sacked out in our queen-size bed. Luke fell asleep first. It must have been all those quilt shops that lulled him into dreamland. I lay nestled in his arms and wondering what I had done to deserve such happiness.

The next chilly morning we made languorous love under a feather quilt. The big decision was to not make any plans. Luke showered and said he'd meet me downstairs. We both decided to take a day off from jogging. There was too much to do.

When I met Luke in the dining room, he was attacking a large plate of Belgian waffles with strawberries and whipped cream.

"Okay, choose between the sex and this breakfast. What's better?" I said.

"Woman, don't mess with me."

I opted for the 7-grain blueberry pancakes and a glass of tomato juice.

"What do you think, should we just move in here?" Luke said with a dab of whipped cream tucked into the corner of his mouth.

"I think Charo is going to be mighty upset if I mention any of this," I said as I took my napkin and dabbed at Luke's mouth.

"Do you know what I think, Babe?"

"Lay it on me."

"I think you and I do pretty great in about any environment," Luke said planting a kiss on my forehead.

And I think I am the luckiest woman in the world.

Back to Reality

After two other delightful bed and breakfast inns, rock climbing, hiking, boating, horseback riding, canoeing and a fall foliage wagon ride, we had had enough of over the river and through the woods and were on a flight back to LAX.

Luke was going to his home and I would catch a flight to Palm Springs.

"It's hard for this to end," I said.

"Babe, think of it as a beginning. We've been through a lot of things in this short time we've been together, and other than your racist, mother-fucking remarks, we be good."

"You put it that way and I guess I have to tell you that I've missed Mr. Silverman horribly."

"Well, you don't think I'm not itching to get my arms around Miss Daisy?"

"So it sounds to me like we're both not sure if we or the pets come first."

"Let's not even consider discussing this," Luke said, "because I hate to see grown women cry."

"Will you be at Heave for the Halloween party? Of course, Miss Daisy is expected, too."

"Tell me we don't have to wear costumes," Luke said.

"You know you do and don't try to get out of it."

"Do you have anything in mind?"

"Look, don't worry about it, I'll have Sam come up with something."

"Please God, don't let it be a two-piece bathing suit or anything with white sheets," Luke said.

The Goddess picked me up at the airport. It was 3:00 p.m. and I was exhausted but exhilarated to be back in the beautiful desert. I wanted to kiss the ground when we landed.

I was too tired to say much on the ride home, so the Goddess regaled me with her plans to turn local cemeteries into venues for special events.

"Look, they're a resting place for major celebrities— Frank Sinatra, Frank Capra, Sony Bono—could go on and on. Why shouldn't people stroll the grounds and remember the greats. We could project some of their films on a mausoleum wall. We're talking history. Or value added if you want to be crass. Think of seeing *From Here to Eternity* with Frank Sinatra's grave nearby. And what about *Mr. Smith Goes to Washington* during an election year? You gotta love it. I'm thinking themed picnic baskets, but I haven't got that worked out yet. Maybe Charo has a few ideas," The Goddess said.

"Should I think of this as life after Wall Street?"

"More like my resurrection," The Goddess said.

When I got home, Mr. Silverman was inside fast asleep on the couch along with a young boy I hoped was Nathan. I tiptoed in so I wouldn't wake them. Next I went into the bedroom to call Luke and tell him I arrived home safely.

"What's the loneliest you've ever been, Babe?"

"Easy question, the time I bought a wooden back scratcher."

"Wrong answer."

"Okay, how about when I would see a bicycle built for two?"

"You're approaching three strikes."

"Okay, okay, my real answer is when you're not next to me," I said.

"Babe, go to the head of the class. It's only been a few hours and I miss you already."

I hung up and saw the sweetest little boy standing in my bedroom doorway.

"Hi, Nathan, do you remember me? I'm Maebeth, your grandmother's friend."

"Yes, ma'am, Silvie and I have been watching your house."

I patted the bed and motioned for him to come sit beside me. He took a running leap and plopped down hard next to me.

"So, have you met any of the ladies here at Heave?" I said.

"Oh, yes, ma'am, Miss Desiree is so pretty and Lady Goddess is so beautiful. Miss Charo is always giving me cookies and Miss Carmen lets me help her plant flowers. I like playing with Sue at Miss Julie's and Beau is neat, but Silvie I like best."

"Well, Silvie is yours anytime you want. Now let's go say hello to your grandmother."

Lily was in her kitchen and looked much better than the last time I saw her. We hugged and then she put her hands on her hips and asked if Nathan was bothering me.

"Oh, Lily, I can see he's been great with Mr. Silverman. Okay, if I give him $5 for his cat sitting?"

Lily squinted and nodded.

Nathan beamed.

"Grandma, I'm going to play out by the pool."

"Remember not to get too close to the edge," Lily said.

When he went out the back door, I went to Lily and put my arms around her again.

"Oh, Maebeth, I'm so glad you're back. It's just not the same here without you. Hope you didn't mind having Nathan in your house, but all of the ladies have kinda adopted him and given him free rein to go into their units."

"He seems pretty content," I said.

"Who knows how much the little guy is hurting. I have enrolled him in school and he'll start next week. It will be good for him to have a routine and be around children his own age."

"I have a feeling Nathan is going to be good for all of us," I said.

"And, thank heavens Sam is here so he has some male reference," Lily said.

"Speaking of Sam, how is he adjusting?" I asked.

"Maebeth, he fits right in. Now he's fussing about the Halloween party and Carmen seems to have loads of projects for him. She's also helping him find a small storefront in Palm Desert where he can get a design studio going."

"Carmen must be in heaven. Well, I need to unpack. I'll catch up with you later."

"I'll be needin' all the details about the foliage and the stud," Lily said, snapping me on the rear with a dishtowel.

"Lily, I don't know if you're old enough to hear about this kind of unbridled sex," I said as I started back home.

I was in the middle of walking out my back door with a bundle of dirty laundry when I ran into Carmen.

"A kiss for the sis," she said.

"Settle for a smile, my hands are full."

"So, you two set a date?"

"Can't an older woman take a trip with a friend to New England to see the leaves turn without all this speculation?"

"Well, I'm up to my eyeballs in projects what with the party, Sam's business and the fall container pot planting."

I grinned.

"Gee, Carmie, I'd like to help but you can see my hands are full," I said.

"Always the smartass," Carmen said.

"Tell me someone is not just whistlin' 'Dixie,'" I said as Honey came sauntering out of her back door with a Bluetooth tucked into her ear.

"I'm outta here," Carmen said.

Honey was wearing an aqua kimono with slits up the sides. She had two wooden sticks in her hair—no small feat considering she has short hair.

"What's with the Madame Butterfly getup?" I asked.

Honey waved and put a just-a-minute finger to her lips as she launched into the chorus.

I nodded toward The Way of the Cross as I headed over to do my laundry.

Julie was on the treadmill with Sue curled up on the floor next to the machine. When she saw me come in, she flicked the off switch and came over to give me a hug.

"God, it's good to see you, Maebeth. This place has been a zoo. It's hard to keep my tan up with all the activity around the pool. That sister of yours always is looking for volunteers and those two boys, Sam and Nathan, are never still. Look at my stomach. Do you think I've gained weight? I haven't been able to do my laps like I used to."

"Julie, you look terrific and Sue doesn't look like she's missed me a bit, the little bitch."

"We all missed you. You are our anchor, our voice of reason," Julie said.

"Don't start with that talk," I said.

When I had my clothes in the washer, I walked out and could smell something wonderful. Sam was at the grill barbecuing some chicken breasts and had some corn wrapped in foil roasting next to them.

"Well, if it isn't Miss Betty Crocker, Heave's newest resident," I said.

"Get over here and kiss the cook," Sam said. "I thought I'd make dinner for all of us to celebrate the world traveler's return."

"Sounds wonderful. I knew voting you into this beehive was the smartest thing any of us ever did."

"I'm feeling reborn," Sam said as he turned over a chicken breast. "Everyone has been so welcoming and to see my Charo every day is a dream come true. I know this isn't the time but after you get settled back in, I would really like to talk to you about a proposition that I'm considering. You're a good business woman and I just want to get your thoughts without any interruptions."

"Please tell me this isn't anything related to Halloween," I said.

Sam laughed and assured me that he did have a serious side.

Charo heard the laughter and came running out to welcome me home.

"Did I miss anything? Welcome back. How was Robert Frost?" Charo said.

"Feelin' no pain," I said.

We held each other a long time. It was so great to see her. It was so great to be home. Whatever the future held for me, I could never envision giving any of this up.

Honey came out of her unit and walked toward us. Charo did a little Japanese bow and I did a double take.

"What's up with all this?" I asked.

"Konnichiwa, Maebeth," Honey said.

"That's 'good afternoon,'" Charo said.

"Are you out of your mind?" I said.

"Hai, or I wouldn't have gotten into this phone sex business," Honey said. "Actually, I thought this would add an exotic dimension to my work. Anyway, Maebeth, you're looking great. It's good to have you back."

Her Bluetooth must have kicked in because she whispered sayonara and began talking in her Desiree voice.

"She just said 'goodbye,'" Charo said.

That did it. I mumbled I would be back for food and headed in to get the little jars of maple syrup that I had schlepped home for everyone.

The Crossings

The next day I was back to my old routine. Awake at 5:30 a.m. and suited up in gray sweats for a run.

The air was chilly, but I had worked up a sweat by the time I reached The Crossings. I did a double take when I spotted a realtor's For Sale sign out front. I knew the owners were past retirement, but I hadn't an inkling that they were thinking of selling.

The clerk in the general store didn't seem to know much more than the sign said. I paid for my bottle of water and caught my breath sitting on the curb out front.

Things were quiet when I got back home. Of course Charo would be up so I stopped in to catch up since we hadn't a real chance to talk last night.

"Good morning, sweet Maebeth. It's so good to have you back. Things around here just aren't the same when you're not around. How about some scrambled eggs and a homemade blueberry muffin? You're looking a little skinny," Charo said.

"You're on, Charo. Say, what's with the For Sale sign at The Crossings?"

"Oh, Sam's been talking about that for a week. I haven't paid much attention, but he seems to have all the details. Maebeth, I'm trying to think of costumes for Lester and me for Halloween. I was going to go as a pole dancer, but everyone's seen that outfit and I want something different. Any ideas?"

"Well, I'll have to think. We've got some time to figure this out."

I was back home hunkered down to reality at my computer doing some back-invoicing when Sam knocked at my front door.

"Sam, I thought it must be a solicitor since no one ever knocks around here."

"Maebeth, if this is a bad time, just let me know. Like I said last night, I just wanted to run something by you."

"No, go ahead, let me get us some iced tea."

We sat at the kitchen table and Sam reiterated how delighted he was to be out of the New York rat race. He also updated me on how he and Carmen had been looking for places for him to launch his interior design business. He said his heart wasn't really in it, but that Carmen said his talent was too important to waste and that this was what he should be doing.

"Carmen can be very forceful," I said.

"I appreciate her interest, but don't think she has any idea just how long it would take to get an interior design business established."

I nodded.

"I've been thinking about The Crossings. I can see the potential. Maybe it's because I have fresh eyes. People on the freeway need to jump off for gas, restrooms and food. The current owners have managed to make a living over the years by catering to the loyal locals. If someone could market the convenience factor to the freeway folks and add some new twists for the locals, it might just be a going concern. I'm thinking I or some of us might have ourselves an opportunity here to have some fun and make a little money," Sam said catching a breath.

His enthusiasm was catching. He went on to say that he had spoken to the realtor and felt it was doable. He also wondered if anyone at Heave would want to be a part of it.

His thought was that if the seven other residents would put in $20,000 each, they could be part owners. Sam, of course, would carry the bulk of the financial burden.

The whole thing sounded intriguing to me and I told Sam that we'd have a meeting and throw out the idea to everyone.

The next afternoon the eight of us and Nathan got together at The Way of the Cross.

Charo had mixed up a pitcher of screwdrivers telling us all that no one should make any big decisions with a clear head, because if they did no risks would ever be taken. There was chocolate milk for Nathan.

Carmen huffed that it wasn't even two o'clock and it certainly was too early for cocktails.

Much to my amusement, Sam poured her a drink and told her to relax.

Sam laid out his plan. The Crossings consisted of a run-down general store, a gas pump and a café. And he added that the property was five acres with lots of room for expansion. He outlined the potential of attracting the Interstate traffic as well as the locals. Sam said he didn't want to pressure anyone. He just wanted to see what the ladies at Heave thought of the idea. He also explained his own situation and that he would still do interior design on a smaller scale, but had yearned for something fresh. What did we think?

The Goddess said she thought the idea had potential. She was convinced that the area would be built up in the next decade and that available land was becoming scarce, thanks to LA and Orange County residents who had had it with their commutes, smog and crime.

Lily said that it would be great if they didn't have to travel so far for everything. And wouldn't it be wonderful if there was an outdoor market where local farmers could sell their stuff. Maybe it could even have an organic foods section.

Charo jumped in and said that the current café was a disgrace and what if it became famous for something like fresh baked pies. She added she knew the perfect person who could bake them every day.

Julie ranted about the price of gas and how with a few more pumps they could accommodate the pending growth.

Honey had moved to the corner of the room and was chatting on her Bluetooth.

I was the last to speak and said that with a few billboards and some Internet presence I thought we could capture some Interstate business. The local business would benefit from word of mouth and a few special promotions.

Sam had been quiet the whole time. I don't think he anticipated the ideas or the enthusiasm. His face was flushed and I could tell he was thrilled.

"Sam, how much would you need from each of us to help you with this enterprise?" I asked.

Sam said he would carry the load, but $20,000 from each of us seven would get the ball rolling.

Everyone started to talk at once.

"Let's everyone have another screwdriver and sleep on it," I said.

Honey returned, hiked up her kimono and sat down on a chair looking confused.

"That was Lenny," she said.

"Jesus," Carmen said as she and Sam hightailed it out the door. Sam already had a victory cigar hanging out of his mouth.

"Should I call Luke for another mano-a-mano session with that weasel?" I said.

"Maybe he's jonesing for another pole dance," Charo said.

The Goddess groaned.

"Oh, lawdy," Lily said.

"Oh, my, I know he's a bastard but he's my bastard. Anyway, he's not coming out here, but he sounded so different. He's found God and is preaching now at prisons trying to set bad guys straight," Honey said.

"Tell that piece of crap 'Vaya con Dios,'" I said with my hands on my hips.

"That's cold," Honey said as she gathered up her kimono and headed for the door.

Tough being the gatekeeper here.

Trick or Treat

The day of the Halloween extravaganza had finally arrived. I headed out for my run knowing this would likely be the quietest time of the day for me.

Mr. Silverman was already back home and waiting in front of Lily's door for his buddy Nathan. What a Benedict Arnold!

It was a gorgeous nippy fall morning and I was excited about seeing Luke. Micha and Frank were also coming and so were Lucy and Mel Bergmann.

Everyone was keeping their costumes secret. And, everyone refused to dress up their animals and I totally agreed.

My outfit was an Elizabethan number I picked up at a costume shop in Palm Springs. I was going as Lady Maebeth and hoped I could get some cleavage out of an old Wonderbra I had stashed in my lingerie drawer.

I usually wasn't into this madness but The Goddess' enthusiasm was contagious. And not knowing what Luke would be wearing was driving me nuts.

When I got to The Crossings, I noted that the For Sale sign now sported an In Escrow banner.

I smiled.

The vote had been unanimous. For most of us this was a chunk of dough, but none of us were into bequeathing. The consensus was to enjoy life and this could be a lot of fun.

I purchased my bottle of water and secretly hoped that I would run into Luke heading for Heave, but he had said it would be afternoon before he could get there. The Bergmanns came in Friday and were making a weekend out of it staying with some friends in Palm Springs while the Sellars would be bunking in at Monistat 1 and arriving today.

I went straight to Charo's when I got back and could smell the waffles before I got to her door. Julie and Sue were already there.

"I need to get my laps in before it gets crazy around here," Julie said scarfing down a large piece of waffle.

"Isn't there some rule about not eating before you swim?" I asked.

"I think that's an old wives' tale and anyway I have my water jogger vest on."

I slipped Sue a piece of waffle and caught Charo giving me a signal that she needed to speak to me in private.

When Julie left, Charo ushered me into her bedroom where a French maid's outfit, complete with a white lacy apron and hat, black fishnet hose and feather duster were laid out on the bed.

"Here's my problem, Maebeth. It's the darn shoes. I can't wear spikes because I'll be workin' the food station and runnin' in and out. But I think white tennis shoes will ruin the look."

Playing it safe while I took a moment to think, I asked Charo what Lester was planning on wearing.

"Oh, he's going to be in a butler getup," Charo said. "We thought we'd look like a good pair. Got the forbidden sex thing goin'."

"Okay, I think I've solved your problem. I hear there will be a fogger around the food station. That low, smoky action will hide your shoes."

"You're a genius! I feel better already," Charo said.

I left through her back door and could see that Sam and Carmen were already at it. Julie was still doing her laps, but surrounding the pool were pumpkins, orange glow sticks, skeletons, a grim reaper tombstone, bats, an inflatable owl, a box of spiders and cobwebs and a grinning skull set that I was told lights up. There was also a stereo setup for all the spooky audio tapes and, thank heavens, the fog machine.

"You two sure have the touch," I said as I headed back to my unit at a fast clip hoping I wouldn't get roped into the decorating.

At any of these fiestas we all were given specific jobs, but everyone generally pitched in when they were needed.

Carmen usually felt it was easier, faster and better if she did things herself, but now she gladly switched gears with Sam's presence.

She was still a little unsettled about Sam's decision to forego opening an interior design shop, but Sam had placated her with the promise to freshen up her unit with some paint, window treatment and a few new pieces.

I was straightening up the kitchen when Honey appeared in a nun's habit. She had the veil on that completely hid her hair and she was wearing flimsy powder blue baby dolls.

"So, you're going as a schizo?" I said.

She bristled.

"No, I am going as a nun. I need a break from this sex thing. Thought I'd try to work into the role. I'm only planning to work a half day today. This could be a new direction for me. Kind of a goody two shoes thing—think librarian, parochial school girl, spinster."

"So what happened to geisha girl?" I said.

"Maebeth, I just couldn't get into exotic. Couldn't get the sing-songy accent going and don't let anyone tell you those kimonos are comfortable. You can hardly breathe with that big sash around your waist and silk just doesn't breathe in the desert."

"Honey, I'm not religious, but let's not be whistling 'Amazing Grace' today. We have children here and we're expecting guests so we need to be sensitive."

"How about 'Rock of Ages?'"

"Sister Desiree, I hope you're kidding."

There was a knock on the back door and it was Nathan. Great, now I had to explain Honey's outfit in a sane way to him.

Honey patted him on the head as she left and Nathan hopped up on a kitchen chair and asked if Silvie was sleeping.

I kissed his forehead.

"Nathan, do you know what the word 'nocturnal' means?"

He shook his head.

I explained the rudiments of cat rituals and asked if he was excited about the Halloween party.

He said he had trouble sleeping, he was so excited. Best of all, he had a new friend from school and he and his dad were coming to the party.

Nathan was going to be Superman and his friend Jose was going to be a Power Ranger.

Hopefully, that would balance out the French maid and the nun that I'd seen so far.

After Nathan left I continued my cleaning and then headed for the shower. It felt great to get the morning run and dust off me and wrapped in a big fluffy towel I headed for the bedroom where Luke was setting down his duffel bag and hanging a suit bag in the closet.

We both had big grins.

"Babe, once again, you are so considerate. This is going to save me some time," he said as we wrapped his arms around me and playfully tugged at the towel.

"Look, I've just spent the morning with a nun and a child. I don't know what kind of girl you think I am."

"Sounds like a research project," Luke said.

About 40 minutes later he knew exactly what kind of girl I am.

Reluctantly, we got out of bed, showered and put on some sweats until we had to dress for the party. I was in charge of setting up the bar and the apple-bobbing corner and I needed to get moving or risk the wrath of big sis.

Luke headed down to see the other woman. I figured he was probably hungry after our workout, so Charo would be able to whip something up for him. Hopefully, she wouldn't be donning the French maid outfit just yet.

Micha joined me at the pool. She and Frank had made themselves at home in Monistat 1. I asked her to run back and tell Frank that Luke was down at Charo's.

The pool area was starting to look like a Haunted House. Nathan was beside himself checking out all the décor. He and Sam had bonded and Sam had put him to work spreading cobwebs. It was wonderful to see the little guy having some joy in his life. Maybe he was young enough not to be too scarred by the tragedy.

Honey was testing the sound system. She was now in full costume and I had to admit it lent a little serenity to the scene. Albeit, a missal in one hand and a bourbon in the other was confusing.

Time to go in and suit up for Lady Maebeth. Hopefully, I could get dressed before Luke returned. I had just laced up the killer bodice and was fluffing out the huge skirt when Luke walked into the bedroom.

"Double trouble, double trouble," he said honing in on the breasts I had just grown.

"Down boy, I think it's 'Double double, toil and trouble; Fire burn and caldron bubble' if I remember correctly."

"You look terrific, Babe!"

"Okay, so let's check out your costume."

"Not a chance. I'll see you out there. I want it to be a surprise."

That's weird.

I was making last minute touches in the bar area when Julie and Moe came out. Julie, dressed in a fringy chemise with a cloche hat, boa and long cigarette holder, was in charge of the Best Costume Contest and was arranging papers at the judges' card table. Moe boasted a wide lapel, double-breasted, pinstripe suit with spectator shoes and a felt fedora. I'm not sure if they were Bonnie and Clyde or a generic gangster and gun moll.

Nathan was racing around trying to fly like Superman.

Mademoiselle Charo and a very proper looking Lester were arranging food platters on a large table in front of The Way of the Cross. The fog machine hadn't yet been turned on but a floor length tablecloth masked the sneakers.

Lily arrived dressed as a sexy aerobics instructor. Her long legs sported Spandex black pants and a red low cut tank top with a matching red headband. She escorted Jose and his father, Manuel, out to the pool. Nathan darted over and high-fived the Power Ranger while Lily began introducing Manuel, who was wearing a Snoopy getup.

Sam was wearing a white chef's jacket and said he was Emeril Lagasse. It was a reach, but when he kept shouting "bam" everyone got it.

"Bam back at you," I said.

The Goddess was flying around in a jet black witch's outfit that included a pointed hat that must have been two-feet tall. Her date, Chris, was a jockey with a twist. He got the helmet, pants, boots, and whip right—but underneath the open green and white silk shirt, he was wearing a matching silk bra.

Moe Capone took one look and headed over for a conversation.

I continued to circulate.

The costume wasn't much of a stretch for Frank Sellars who was wearing a cop's blues, while Micha had on black and white horizontal striped pants, shirt and hat and was his jailbird.

The Bergmanns arrived and were precious as Sonny and Cher. Miss Daisy was with them and making herself at home with Nathan and Jose.

I was about to see what was up with Luke when the spooky noises were replaced with the theme from "Rocky."

Out of my back door danced Luke with a white satin robe piped in black and "Rocky" written in bold letters on the back and a roomy hood over his head. He was jabbing rights and lefts with red boxing gloves.

"Shut your mouth," Carmen said. Not exactly the sweetest remark from someone dressed as Alice in Wonderland.

Everyone roared with laughter and clapped as Luke continued to skip around the perimeter of the pool, feinting punches. Miss Daisy had figured out who this was and was chasing after him and jumping up and down.

Luke tore off his robe and now was in white satin trunks.

Bless me, father, for I have sinned.

Finally, the music stopped and Luke came over and gave me a big hug.

"We just couldn't resist having some fun with you, Babe."

I grinned.

"Jeez, a black Rocky."

"Hey, this is all they had that would fit."

Luke patted Miss Daisy on the head and said he thought he'd like to see me bob for apples in my Elizabethan clothes.

This was going to be some evening and, by god, I was going to be comfortable.

"Thanks for reminding me," I said as I headed back to my unit to change.

When I returned, I had replaced the bodice with an orange sweatshirt that had *Boo Hoo* on the front.

I was making the rounds and noticed that Manuel couldn't take his eyes off of Lily.

I went up to Lily and asked, "What's with your friend, Snoopy?"

"I don't know, Maebeth. Every time I jiggle my keys he comes over here panting. I'd take him for a ride in the car, but he'd probably drool and hang his head out the window."

"Well, girlfriend, he's interested and he's cute."

"He's a teacher at Nathan's school, so we do have that in common. I hear he married a woman 25 years younger than he and she got bored and left the child."

"I'd throw him a biscuit if I were you," I said.

As the evening wore on, the Best Costumes Award went to Nathan and Jose.

On accepting the award from Julie, Jose said, "Sweet."

Nathan, ever the gentleman said, "Thank you, ma'am."

Honey was passed out on a chaise with her veil inched down to her eyebrows. Charo and Lester were putting cake and corn candy into little bags for guests to take home. I was looking forward to a few rounds in the boxing ring.

One by one we said our goodbyes and assumed our real identities until next year.

Rebirth

The Crossings now belonged to all of us at Heave. Initially, we planned no changes in staffing, although Sam was on site most of the day.

I was working on a mini-market marketing plan. We didn't want to begin any advertising until we made some changes and had something to promote.

There was a lot of discussion about changing the name. This seemed to be a sound idea in that we could incorporate the new owners, new look, new features to our dual market.

"Heathens" was one suggestion. I liked the play off Heave, but was concerned it would be construed as an adult bookstore and offend the sensitive patrons.

"Heaven-sent" got serious consideration. Everyone felt this was a heaven-sent opportunity for Heave residents as well as for locals and travelers. It was finally decreed to name our new adventure: "Heaven-sent at The Crossings."

Now the real work would begin.

The restaurant concept was next on the list. Sam felt we needed to work with the cook and find out what was popular before we made any changes. He was leaning toward a diner ambiance with comfort food. Charo introduced her homemade pies to the menu. She started out with two pumpkin and two banana crème. In addition we ordered individual slice pie boxes for the to-go crowd. Sam made a cute sign announcing Charo's Famous Homemade Pies.

And speaking of signs, we had a new one with our new name on order. That alone would be a big improvement over the crooked, faded sign that had been up forever.

The restrooms were in bad shape and were to be retiled and fitted with new sinks and toilets. The Men's Room was already being worked on while Les Dames would have to double for both sexes.

Lily had chosen a warm mustard color for the interior of the café and general store. She would be doing the painting on weekdays and on weekends Manny would join her and help with the exterior, which was going to be sage and would look good with the adobe tile roof.

After discussion with Carmen, a landscaper was hired to update the flowers and shrubs around the exterior and to clear the tumbleweeds off the acreage.

Once that had been accomplished we decided to pave a large section next to the general store, which would be the venue for a farmers market, swap meet and maybe even a fiesta.

Carmen was taking an inventory of the general store and reviewing what needed to be tossed and what needed to be introduced. She wanted to add postcards and souvenirs for the tourists along with sundries and basics for locals who lamented the inconvenience of markets not being close by.

Now that we had a new name and logo, I got busy working with a graphic designer on billboards. We also agreed to run a series of 8½ x 11 inserts targeted to the east valley in *The Desert Sun's* neighborhood tabloid.

Heaven-sent was a beehive of activity and energized us all.

More Changes

Honey came through my back door as I was mixing up a salmon salad. Mr. Silverman took a break from his snooze to rub against my leg. Guess salmon beats sleep anytime.

I put the empty can of salmon down on the kitchen floor and did a double take at Honey who looked horrible. She was wrapped tight in a ratty flannel robe and was blowing her nose into a Kleenex.

"Bad cold?" I asked.

I could barely make out, "I'm miserable. Can't work and the phone is going crazy. Can anyone here help me out?"

"Don't look at me. Carmen was good at this. Maybe she can help. And what about Charo? She'd love sit in for you."

I phoned Carmen and there was no answer. Must be at Heaven-sent.

Charo was home and said she'd be right over but first needed to change her clothes.

This could be scary.

In 10 minutes she came tearing through the back door dressed in a black Spandex pantsuit.

"Let's get started," Charo said to Honey who was sipping a mug of hot tea.

"What do you think of this outfit? Got inspired when I saw Lily at the Halloween party in that aerobics getup. It was the bomb."

Honey began instructing her on the nuances of the Bluetooth.

"What about the whistlin'? Should I throw that in, too?"

It was decided that she should introduce herself as Desiree's associate since regular customers would pick up on the voice and style.

"I'm going to be Cerise. That's a pretty sexy name," Charo said.

I walked toward the door and opened it.

"Ladies, can you take this out of here. I have some work to do. Honey, I'll be over later with some chicken soup. Try to get some rest."

As I was sweeping off my front porch, Lily came out with Beau. "We're going for a walk, want to join us?"

We started for Heaven-sent.

"My, my, Maebeth, I just can't imagine what my life has turned into to. Why, in just a few months I have buried my beautiful son and gotten so attached to his wonderful child. Now my days are filled with baking cookies, homework, soccer and all the other things I did 30 years ago. And then there's Manny. What in the world am I supposed to do with him?"

"Did that old dog throw you a bone yet?" I said.

"Oh, lawdy, he's actually pretty hot. I don't think you've really taken a good look at him since he got out of the Snoopy suit. It's nice taking the kids to movies and out to eat. It's nice to have someone to do things with. I haven't felt like this for a long time. Manny and I have so much in common with these kids."

"That's wonderful, Lily, but I thought Nathan was only going to be with you for the school year and then he would go live with Iggy and Dennis."

"That's what we thought of initially when none of us was thinking clearly. Now some time has gone by and I'm not so sure. The boys will be here for Thanksgiving so we will have a good talk then about Nathan's best interests."

When we got to Heaven-sent, Carmen was busy stocking shelves in the general store. I told her about Honey's condition and that she could use some assistance in that I wasn't sure how Charo would work out.

"Hey, let's call Cerise and see how she's working out? Oh, bad idea, Sam is the only male voice we have here and it would be beyond creepy to have his grandmother talk to him like that," I said.

We put a bowl of water down on the road for Beau. Lily and I sat on the curb nursing our bottled waters.

"Would you ever consider leaving Heave?" I asked.

"Would you?"

"The old answer the question with a question trick. There are times all I can think of is being with Luke. And then when I'm away from Heave—like when we were leaf peepers a little while ago—I return home and know how much I love my girlfriends and what a great life this is."

"I feel the same way," Lily said. "I know what a man can bring into your life, but I also know how much work that is. Being at Heave just feels so right. When Slinky was sick I marveled how we all stayed close. Then we were able to move on and welcome Sam. We seem to gather strength from each other and it's such an amazingly strong bond that we all have even though we are all so different."

Amen, sista.

Dennis and Iggy

It is the day before Thanksgiving. Lily and Nathan have gone to the Palm Springs International Airport to pick up Dennis and Iggy.

This year Thanksgiving is to be held at Heaven-sent's café which was closed for the holiday. Sam was fussing over the preparations and Carmen was having a great time checking off the list of what had been accomplished.

Luke, Lester, Chris, Moe, Manny, Jose and the Sellars were all coming. None, except Luke, had seen the progress we had all made at Heaven-sent. The gas station area had been upgraded and now consisted of two pumps. A large orange and white striped canopy shaded most of the outdoor concrete floor that had been poured. Both the inside and exterior had been painted and the new neon sign was standing proud.

There was still a lot to be done, but we had accomplished a great deal in a short time.

Luke and I were stretched out on chaises out by the pool enjoying the warm sun on our faces. It was too chilly to sunbathe so we both relaxed in our jeans and jackets, sipping Arnold Palmers with not a care in the world. The pool was heated for diehards, which we were not.

Lily was back because Nathan darted out her back door and took a running leap for Luke's lap. There was no doubt that the two were crazy about each other. Nathan had taken to wearing his ball cap sideways and it was a running joke that every time he walked by one of the sisters at Heave, or our friends, we would right the cap.

He was a great kid and coming into his own trying to seek an identity. A few times he had come home from school with some of his clothes torn. Manny was keeping an eye on him as best he could, but the truth was that Nathan was one of the few black kids at the school and, indeed, kids can be cruel.

"Hey, sport, what are you up to?" Luke said, straightening Nathan's cap.

"We got company. They're going to take me to Disneyland this weekend. And they said Jose could come, too."

"Did they say they'd take me, too?" Luke asked.

"Nope, but I can ask."

"Oops, I just remembered I promised Maebeth I would take her to the movies."

The two boys were doing a little light wrestling when Dennis and Iggy came out. Both Luke and I had met them at the funeral and were very impressed at how they handled everything and their devotion to each other.

"Hey, don't mess with my man," Dennis said.

"Hey, yourself. Someone should be protecting me against this wild kid," Luke said.

Luke gently removed Nathan from his lap and got up to shake hands. I added warm hugs to the welcome, invited them to stretch out and went in to get them both some drinks.

I returned just as Chris was exiting The Goddess' back door in his famous two-piece.

The two newcomers were speechless.

"Let me do the introductions. Dennis and Iggy, meet Chris, a friend of The Goddess," I said.

"Goddess?" Iggy asked.

"Get used to it, Iggy. You're in for a wild ride. This place makes Disneyland boring," Luke said.

I grinned.

"Nice to meet you both. Any of you interested in a swim? It's warm in the pool and if you've been traveling it's a good way to stretch those big muscles you're both sporting," Chris said.

"Well, we do have our suits inside. Want to go California, Iggy?" Dennis asked.

"Let's do it," said Iggy, heading for Monistat 1.

"Babe, it's great to have some Y chromosomes around here," Luke said.

"Well, I'm not too sure if they're all Y, if you know what I mean."

Luke nodded.

Nathan joined the guys in the pool along with a bunch of inflatable rafts and toys he pulled from The Way of the Cross.

Luke and I watched them all play for a while and then went over to see what Charo was up to.

Honey walked in, Bluetooth tucked into her ear, whistling "Mack the Knife." She was wearing a bright red velour leisure suit with two-inch long red, glass-beaded earrings and red high heels. Good to know she was taking better care of herself. Her bad cold has cost her some bucks and Charo, or should I say Cerise, didn't work out as her assistant. Guess softly reciting recipes didn't cut it with Desiree's trade.

We were meeting the Sellars in Palm Desert for dinner. Since Monistat 1 was occupied, they were staying at The Embassy Suites.

I went back home to catch a nap and anything else I could before we had to leave. Luke had left Charo's earlier and was snoring lightly while sprawled out on the couch. I turned off the TV. By 6:00 p.m. I awoke refreshed and could hear the shower running.

Luke came back into the bedroom with a towel wrapped around his waist. As I was tugging out of my oversized sweatshirt, he came over and put his arms around me. There was time. There was always time for this wonderful man.

Turkey Day

As was the tradition at Heave, Thanksgiving morning was always spent at the local rescue mission helping prepare for their noon meal. Today, they expected more than 300 folks who were down on their luck.

The chefs at The Westin Mission Hills Resort had for many years cooked and delivered turkeys. Various local restaurants helped with the pumpkin pies and trimmings. Grocery stores also donated boxes of canned and packaged foods. These items were packed in individual cartons and later delivered to needy families.

The ladies at Heave were among many volunteers who started their Thanksgiving at the mission. Today, Luke, Dennis, Iggy and Nathan joined us. Sam and Carmen stayed behind to finish their work at the café.

When our work was finished and everyone was fed, we walked out to our cars to head home for a rest before we had our own celebration.

I was in the parking lot with Charo and Luke when I heard a scream. It was Honey flailing about with her hands in the air and running in circles.

"Oh, shit. Shit, shit, shit," Honey yelled. "Somebody stole my car."

Luke went into cop mode.

"Are you sure you parked it in this spot?" Luke said.

Honey was hysterical and not whistling a happy tune. Her 2005 white Toyota Camry LE was her baby. This would not be considered a luxury car in an area where a Bentley, Rolls and Lexus were commonplace, but for Honey it was the culmination of a lot of hard work and it was paid for in full.

"Hell yes. I was parked right here."

Luke dialed the police on his cell. Julie and The Goddess had driven with Honey and were trying to calm her down.

Since there was nothing they could do, everyone squeezed into the SUV Dennis and Iggy had rented while Luke and I waited with Honey for the police to arrive.

"Calm down, Honey, we're doing all we can do," I said.

"I'm sorry, Maebeth, I just loved that car."

It only took about 10 minutes for Indio's finest to arrive. The cop looked fine in a uniform. Muscular, late 40s, blond and tan.

Honey in a breathless stage whisper said, "Holy shit, Maebeth, is he too cute or what?"

"I can see you're feeling better," I said.

Luke was oblivious as he introduced himself and explained the situation to Sgt. Brad Stephens.

While the paperwork was being completed, Honey fished out a pink business card and handed it to the officer. I hoped it wasn't advertising Desiree's services.

The officer looked a little flustered as Honey wiped a tear from her eye and thanked him for being so understanding about her "little ole Toyota."

After we got back to Heave, there wasn't much time to do anything but change clothes and drive over to Heaven-sent.

Sam and Carmen had knocked themselves out. There were pumpkins, dried flowers and fall decorations everywhere. Two servers passed around Goat Cheese Tortas and champagne. For Nathan and Jose, there was sparkling apple cider. A buffet table took up one side of the room and featured a traditional spread of roast turkey and stuffing, green beans, garlic mashed potatoes, sweet potato casserole, cranberry relish and butter rolls.

The dessert table boasted Pecan and Pumpkin Pies along with an ornate sign that read Charo's Famous Homemade Pies. Trust Carmen to have included recipe cards on the table for people to take home.

Honey's stolen vehicle was the major topic of conversation.

Everyone, even Honey, was in high spirits and as I looked around the room, I marveled at how blessed I was to have all of these beautiful people in my life. If there is anything good about getting older, it is how we treasure those close to our heart and appreciate every minute we have with them. Slinky Rue had taught us all how short life is and how to live it well and exit with dignity.

"Here's to our beloved Slinky," I said as we clinked our champagne flutes.

The Day After

Luke and I got up early Friday morning to jog off the sins of yesterday. My sweatshirt today was apropos and read *Miss Piggy Rocks*.

"Buttercup, you're running like you forgot to step away from the buffet," I said.

"About that shirt, Miss Piggy."

Both of us were feeling the after effects of the previous day. Heaven-sent already had one customer at a gas pump when we arrived. Inside, the café was open and ready for business with a few who looked like tourists having breakfast.

We were paying for our water when we overheard the lady with the group ask the waiter if she could have a whole pecan pie to go. She went on to say they had been visiting relatives in Indio and their Thanksgiving Dinner desert was a pecan pie that their hostess had said came from Heaven-sent. It was in her words "to die for" and "the best she's ever had." She said the reason they stopped by on their way home was to pick one up. She asked if there was any way they could order pies by mail. She knew her friends in Phoenix would want to try them.

"Oh, Luke, did you hear that?" I asked. "I can't wait to tell Charo."

"Lord knows that sweet woman deserves all the accolades. She is one fine cook."

Luke and I went straight to Charo's to tell her the news and to let her twist our arms about breakfast. I grabbed a piece of toast and headed home while Luke stayed on with his other girlfriend.

As I passed Carmen's unit, she yelled out for me to come in. Tonight's entertainment was to be The Goddess' first foray into cemetery cinema. We were all to go out to the Coachella Valley Cemetery where Frank Capra and his wife, Lucille, were buried. The movie on the mausoleum wall was to be *It's a Wonderful Life.* It was thought to be the perfect film to usher in the holiday season. I was still trying to recover from Thanksgiving, so this all felt a little premature to me.

"What do you think of this picnic?" Carmen asked.

She was assembling cardboard bakery boxes and inserting turkey sandwiches, baked potato chips, carrot strips, olives and pickles. Beer, wine and soft drinks would also be carted out to the cemetery. She had packages of snowball cakes for dessert and asked if I thought this was festive enough. I said maybe some Christmas ribbon around the boxes would help with the holiday theme.

"Smashing," Carmen said.

Everyone was to bring blankets and light-weight lawn chairs as well as flashlights.

Lily and Nathan would not be going. Lily felt it was way too early for either of them to be cavorting around the dead. And Nathan needed his rest for tomorrow was Disneyland.

On the other hand, Charo's daughter Sarah was buried in this cemetery and she already had purchased a holiday wreath to place on her grave.

Most of our day was spent reading, napping and not eating. A languorous, long weekend was what we both seemed to need.

If truth be known, I had always hated the holidays. I feel they can play way too much on syrupy emotion. This was one of the reasons the ladies of Heave took a trip each December.

Personally, I loved to tell the story of how as a young girl out of college I used to weep at the Andy Williams' Christmas specials. There was the entire family— smiling, white-haired grandparents, famous singing brothers with white turtle necks peeking out of their colorful ski sweaters and loving wives with their perfectly behaved kids— sitting around a huge crackling fire with a gigantic Christmas tree surrounded with gifts. Jing-a-ling, jing-a-ling, a light lacey snow is falling and here comes smiling Andy in a horse-drawn carriage with his beautiful wife, Claudine, and their exquisite children. Petite Claudine is giggling while whispering sweet nothings to Baby Williams with that soft little girlish French accent. They enter the chalet and it's hugs and kisses for everyone. Cut to the kid's bedroom where Andy and Claudine are crooning a lullaby to the perfect baby. More proof that my life with no boyfriend and spending the holiday season in a dingy studio apartment was total crap.

Then I read about the divorce and next that Claudine wiped out her Olympic skier boyfriend Spider Sabich with a gunshot. In was 1976 and my year of redemption.

That was one great lesson in if it's too good to be true, it usually is.

But snuggled up in a blanket with Luke watching Jimmy Stewart and Donna Reed, I hoped that all wonderful things were not too good to be true.

I was trying to get into a comfortable position when I turned on my side and spotted Honey a couple blankets down, feeding olives to a blond guy who looked very familiar.

"Luke, check out Honey's date, who does he look like?"

"Hmmm, hot damn, that'd be the good officer Stephens," Luke said stifling a chuckle.

"Crissake, Buttercup, wasn't her car just stolen yesterday?"

"We officers of the law don't dally," Luke said.

Sgt. Brad was engrossed in the film when I caught Honey's eye and did a what's-up gesture with my hands and eyes.

Honey mouthed, "I needed a ride."

She'd be getting a ride all right. Yikes, I wondered if Sgt. Brad had any idea of Desiree or of her ex, Lenny.

After the movie The Goddess thanked everyone for coming and was ecstatic about her first program.

All of us then packed our cars up and in a parade of flashlights headed out to find Sarah's grave. After we located it, those of us who knew her well told stories. My story involved my first introduction to Charo. We were at TGI Fridays and Sarah was thrilled I was going to finally meet her mom. Charo looked beautiful with perfectly coiffed hair, a beige pantsuit and matching gold necklace and earrings. Everything was going smoothly until the young waitress was asked by Charo for some sour cream for her baked potato. The waitress clearly took a while to understand what it was Charo was asking and got a little snippy. As she turned on her heel and headed back to the kitchen, tiny, white-haired Charo said, "Shitass."

Sarah sunk her head into her hands and I doubled up with laughter. All of our stories that night touched on the loving and hilarious relationship between mother and daughter. Charo placed the wreath against the headstone and we bowed our heads in silence.

The Weekend

Saturday morning Dennis, Iggy and Nathan were up early. Luke was still sleeping and I tiptoed out to have a coffee with Lily and tell her about last evening.

We sat out on the front porch watching the sun come up and sipping hot coffee.

Lily said that she had had the tough conversation about Nathan's future with Dennis and Iggy. The two had considered adopting before Henry and Ruth were killed. Now here was Nathan looking more like Henry every day. They felt they could provide Nathan with a warm, healthy environment. It was plain that they loved the kid and that Nathan loved them.

"I'm just too old to give that boy everything he needs for a well-rounded life. I'd sure do it if there were no good alternatives, but I think Dennis and Iggy would make wonderful parents. I don't want to disrupt the child any more than we have to so I've suggested Nathan finish out the school term here and then head back with them in the summer," Lily said.

"I think you're doing what's best for the boy, Lily."

Out of the corner of my eye I saw Mr. Silverman heading over my way. He plopped down at my feet.

"That's a new one," I said. "Hope my little man is feeling okay. Look, here comes The Goddess."

As gorgeous as The Goddess was—with or without makeup—she had a

---

thing for the ugliest old lady dusters that snapped up the front. Today she was in an aqua flannel number with pink embroidery on the bodice.

She pulled up a chair and settled in with her mug of tea.

"Good morning, Lily. And, hello, Maebeth. I'm dying to hear your take on last night's screening. I know there are a lot of refinements to be made, but what did you think, overall?"

"We had a great time; however, I did think we could have used a few more lights. It was so dark and I know that's part of the fun in a cemetery, but I do think that could be improved. Also, maybe we could have a little talk before and a Q&A on Frank Capra and his contributions."

The Goddess nodded.

"Great idea. I plan to print programs in the future, but I think comments before the program would be terrific. I'm so excited. I think the potential for something really successful is right here. Why, the celebrities at Desert Memorial Park would boggle your mind," The Goddess said.

"Who's there besides Frank and Sonny?" Lily asked.

"Oh, Betty Hutton, Busby Berkeley, Jolie and Magda Gabor, Brad Dexter, Cameron Mitchell, William Powell and lots of silent screen stars. Besides showing Sonny's *Hairspray* and Frank's *Robin and the 7 Hoods*, there's *Life With Father*, *The Magnificent Seven*, *Annie Get Your Gun*, *The Asphalt Jungle*, *My Man Godfrey*, *The Greatest Show on Earth*— it's endless."

"Wow, I had no idea," I said.

Now The Goddess was warming up. "And we could do a whole thing with epitaphs. Sonny's is: *And the beat goes on.*

"There are tons of hilarious epitaphs. I've been doing some research. Just listen to some of these," The Goddess said as she unfolded a piece of paper that she plucked from her duster pocket.

Here lies Ann Mann,

Who lived an old maid
But died an old Man

Here lies
Johnny Yeast
Pardon me
For not rising.

Here lies the body
Of Jonathan Blacke
Stepped on the gas
Instead of the brake.

Sir John Strange
Here lies an honest lawyer,
And that is Strange.

Here lies Lester Moore
Four slugs from a .44
No Les No More

On the 22nd of June
Jonathan Fiddle
Went out of tune

Bill Blake
Was hanged by mistake.

I would
rather be here
than in Texas.

Here lies the body
Of Margaret Bent
She kicked up her heels
And away she went.

Stranger tread
This ground with gravity.
Dentist Brown
Is filling his last cavity.

Here lies the father of 29,
He would have had more
But he didn't have time.

Here lies the body of Aunt Charlotte.
Born a virgin, died a harlot.
For 16 years she kept her viginity
A damn'd long time for this vicinity.

A bit breathless, The Goddess asked, "What do you think?"

"I think you've found your calling," I said. "You've got yourself a new career."

"Well, Maebeth, I could use your help with some marketing. I'm thinking maybe we could put some flyers on the counter at Heaven-sent. And maybe at the airport and chambers of commerce."

"I'd love to help you out. This will be a fun project," I said as Mr. Silverman jumped off my lap and headed home.

Cat was acting strange.

Lily went in to get us more coffee. The Goddess got up to leave just as Honey approached.

"Well, how's the star of *Carless in Palm Springs*? You certainly know how to get over a trauma. How did you get so well acquainted with the good officer?" I asked.

"Ladies, wouldn't you know Brad stopped by yesterday to give me a report on my Toyota. He asked if my holiday weekend was improving and I told him about the movie at the cemetery and how I was trying to figure out how I would get there. Being the gentleman and good citizen that he is, he offered to escort me."

"I see you're minus your earpiece this morning," Lily said.

Honey nodded.

"Oh, I just had a call from Brad who said he had some news about the car and was coming by to tell me."

"Lawdy, lawdy, us black folks don't get that kind of attention from the police," Lily said.

Just then a black and white pulled up and Honey, looking ever so collegiate in a white polo shirt, khaki slacks and brown loafers went over to greet Sgt. Stephens.

We stared.

Honey waved at us and went into a Paris Hilton trot.

"Where the heck did she get those clothes?" The Goddess said. "I know for a fact there is nothing like that in her closet. I bet she hit up Julie or Carmen for that outfit."

"Well, thank heavens it wasn't her private school costume with the starched cotton blouse with the Peter Pan collar and that painfully short little pleated plaid skirt," I said. "I need to go wake Luke up. He's missing the best part of the day."

Luke was showered, shaved and at my kitchen table with a cup of black coffee and the newspaper.

"What do you say we give Charo the morning off and the three of us drive over to Heaven-sent for breakfast?" I said.

"Great idea, Babe, but it was lonely waking up without you beside me."

"I'll wait until we're seated at breakfast to tell you what you missed. It will take me a minute to get changed."

Beating Charo up in the morning was no small feat, but the late movie caused her to sleep in later than usual. Lester's car was outside so we decided we'd mind our own business and drive over to Heaven-sent by ourselves.

"Are you sure we shouldn't jog over?" I said.

"Might be best if we saved our energy for future activities."

I nodded.

Still feeling fat from all the holiday food, I had chosen *Born to Eat* for today's tee and matched it with a pair of my loosest jeans and a black ball cap.

Sam was already there in his office going over some invoices. He joined us in the café for coffee.

"Sam, we don't see much of you anymore. Is this taking up more of your time than you had hoped?" I asked.

"Maebeth, I've never been happier. I feel reborn. I've already got our first Heaven-sent Farmers Market scheduled for next Saturday. We'll start small at first, but when the word gets out that this is the place for produce, we'll be on the map for sure. We're already doing 10 pies a day. Charo can't do it all, but she's baking what she can, introducing new recipes and supervising our cook so that he can take up the slack. Your billboards have also been drawing in the business. The new gas pumps will soon have paid for themselves. We still haven't figured out what all should go into the general store side. That area still looks a little tired to me and there's nothing less attractive than dusty old merchandise."

"How about a silkscreen tee of Charo eating a slice of one of her famous pies?" I said.

"That's just the kind of creative thinking we need here. Maybe it's time for another meeting with the ladies at Heave," Sam said.

"Well, anyway, Sam, don't work too hard. Carmen is already moping around that you're not spending enough time with her. You know how high maintenance she can be," I said.

"Oh, Carmie is fine. She's all excited that I'm going to help redecorate her unit in Italian modern," Sam said.

"Sounds like fun," I said trying to gather up some enthusiasm. "Carmen really has good taste. More than I can say for her sister."

When we got back to Heave, Honey and The Goddess were pulling out in The Goddess' black BMW. Honey had learned that her car had been totaled and that she'd be needing new wheels. Her insurance was good, but it was the hassle that was dragging her down, and that she was losing a whole day's business. The girls had decided to go to Cathedral City and check out the new cars. As they were driving away, I could hear Honey whistling "YMCA."

"What's this on the floor?" I said.

Luke and I were walking in my front door when I noticed a little puddle of yellow just inside the door. Mr. Silverman had been sick. I found him in the kitchen lying down by his water dish. Hopefully, this was just a fur ball, but he had been looking a little skinnier and I'd noticed his appetite was off. I made a mental note not to panic. I'd just keep a close watch on him and if he didn't improve I'd call my friend Amanda, who had a booming veterinary practice in Indio.

Luke could see that I was distracted. He put his strong arms around me and I rested my head against his chest.

"Buttercup, I don't know what I'd do if anything happened to Mr. Silverman. He's been my best friend for 14 years," I said while hooking a tortoise comb tighter in my hair. "God, I so love that little guy."

I wanted to scoop him up and hold him, but also didn't want to add to his stress. Personally, I understood wanting to be in a corner alone when you're sick. I could never understand people feeling that they had to visit sick friends in the hospital. Hell, it was bad enough having someone drop in unannounced when you're home and well, much less when you're without makeup and your ass is hanging out of a dingy gown and tubes are snaking out of your orifices.

"Maebeth, I do understand what you're feeling. We all have lost pets and it's one of those things in life that doesn't get easier with experience. Maybe, it's just a little malaise, but if it's more serious, then you know I'm here for you and we'll get through this together," Luke said.

We hugged.

Why do you build me up/build me up/Buttercup, baby!

We had planned to go to a movie, but I didn't want to leave Mr. Silverman so we stayed home and snuggled in front of the TV. As the evening wore on, my little guy wanted to go out and I took that for a sign that he was feeling better.

Luke was heading back to LA in the morning and I was starting to miss him already.

Mr. Silverman

Sunday morning we started early worshipping each other's bodies. It was a nice way to end a long holiday weekend and I wasn't sure when we'd see each other next.

The ladies of Heave would be leaving soon for their Mexican Riviera cruise. We had decided years ago that instead of exchanging gifts we'd spend a week away together each December. This would be our first cruise. We had been to dude ranches, spas and Las Vegas.

I took a quick shower, donned my *Witness Protection* tee, which got a second look and a wry grin from Luke. Sweatpants, New Balance running shoes and my black ball cap went well with grandma's ruby earrings.

I went to check on Mr. Silverman while Luke showered and packed up his things. More and more he was traveling light leaving a wardrobe behind, which warmed my heart.

"Is that my little guy?" I said.

Mr. Silverman was waiting by the front door. He started purring when he saw me and then I scooped him up and showered him with kisses. I sat down on the couch with him on my lap and petted him until he dozed off. I carried him into the bedroom and gently placed him on a pillow and tucked a light quilt over him.

Luke and I hit the road at a good stride and I felt I had made inroads on all the damage I'd done over the holiday. Heaven-sent was already doing a brisk breakfast business and there were two cars getting gas for the trip home.

Things were quiet at Heave when we returned. Iggy, Dennis and Nathan were back from Disneyland and I'm sure they were all exhausted. Only Charo was stirring and we walked over so Luke, who was anxious to get on the 10 before the traffic hit, could say his goodbyes. Charo insisted on sending him off with a thermos of coffee and some blueberry muffins. She also had baked two cherry pies—one for Luke and one for the Bergmanns.

Neither of us liked dramatic partings so Luke patted the top of my cap and I slugged him on the arm.

"See ya," I said and I turned and walked back to my unit. Carmen spotted me and came out to say good morning.

Like our dear mother she had a sixth sense that kicked in when something was wrong with any of us.

"You sad because Luke is leaving?"

"Carm, that, but I'm so worried about Mr. Silverman."

I told her what had transpired and she agreed that it was probably nothing. Carmen was great with animals even though Micha's Salt and Pepper were a few more houseguests than she had wanted. She said she'd stop by later to check on my little guy.

Mr. Silverman was sound asleep where I left him. I grabbed a paperback and an iced tea and headed out to the pool. Julie was doing her laps with Sue dozing on a bright yellow beach towel spread over a chaise. Sue was hilarious to watch sleep. Often when she was dreaming she would furiously work her back feet as if in flight. Just a hand on her neck and she would settle down without waking up.

The Goddess was up early and joined me. She had spent a rare evening alone and was clearly confused. Her business was taking some time to get going, but she did have two funerals this week that she was looking forward to. Both involved hair, makeup and post-burial parties.

I needed to take another look at death. For me, the thought of getting too old to take care of myself and then croaking was something to fear. For The Goddess, passing was a celebration.

Maybe there was a cat heaven. Not being religious in spite of a rigorous Catholic upbringing, I had always believed that a kind god would be one who united us with our pets. I didn't give a rat's ass if I ever saw an ex-boyfriend in the next life—in fact I hoped like hell I wouldn't run into any of the sorry bastards. Mr. Silverman was another story. Here again, I differed from The Goddess who kept in close touch with her former husbands (there had been two), boyfriends and lovers. She obviously wasn't Italian.

Honey joined us carrying a tray with four mugs of hot chocolate. She was looking especially chipper, Bluetooth in place and whistling "What a Wonderful World." After the murmurings and heavy breathing was completed, she explained her good mood.

"Sgt. Brad and I are going to dinner and a movie this evening. Isn't that sweet? And I have one of those rare singing gigs in Palm Springs this week and he said he'd love to stop in and hear me."

"Does Riverside County's finest have any idea about your new career?" The Goddess asked.

"I told him it's kind of a reverse telemarketing job that I can do from my home."

"Jeez, Honey, if you two keep seeing each other you're going to have to tell him about Desiree," I said. "And what about Lenny?"

"Maebeth, it's way too early for confession. We're talking about a man, so what he doesn't know won't hurt him. If anything I've learned in this new job, it's that men aren't real complicated," Honey said.

"You didn't need to get into phone sex to understand that. I could have told you that," The Goddess said.

"Maybe that's why I haven't been real successful with men," I said. "I guess

I have given them more credit than they deserve. But then there's Luke and he's nothing like any of the guys I've had the displeasure of knowing."

"Maybe, just maybe, you've gotten wiser," The Goddess said.

This girl totally gets it when it comes to men.

Julie got out of the pool and wrapped herself in a big white terry robe.

"Mmm, hot chocolate. Who made this?" she asked.

"Compliments of Honey Dean," The Goddess said.

"Oh, and that's not the only thing I have for everyone," Honey said. "I got a big Fed Ex box yesterday from Lenny and in it he has a Bible for each of you."

"Praise the Lord," I said.

"What's up with that sicko?" Julie asked.

"Well, I thought I mentioned that Lenny's found God and is going to prisons to spread the word," Honey said.

"He should feel right at home in his workplace," Julie said.

"Oh, I know he's an asshole, but he is trying," Honey said.

"Honey, don't you dare go soft on us. He is persona non gratis at Heave," I said.

The Goddess said, "Maybe, Honey has a point. It's not healthy to hold a grudge. Possibly we should allow him to return to The Way of the Cross and redeem himself in front of all of us."

"Goddess, that is just so much bullshit. You ladies invite that dickweed back and I'm inviting Sgt. Brad," I said.

"Settle down, Maebeth. We're just discussing forgiveness," The Goddess said.

Thank heavens Sam walked out of his unit and joined us. He said that Dennis and Iggy decided to play a round of golf with him before they headed home. After all, with more than 125 golf courses in the Palm Springs area, it would be criminal if they didn't take advantage.

It was interesting to me that The Goddess and Julie were the only golfers at Heave. I could never understand what the big attraction was and I was definitely in the minority.

Julie said, "I read where Mattel had introduced a golf club set for Barbie. I think that's pretty neat. It gives girls another chance to compete in a man's world."

"Personally, Barbie has always pissed me off. To suggest long legs, long blonde hair and a big bust make for the ideal women, sucks," I said.

"Well, when we were young, the most a doll could ever do was wet and cry," Julie said. "It was all about being a mommy and a nurturer. I think it's nice that Barbie is an alternative to that."

"Gotta go," I said.

"Maebeth, you seem out of sorts this morning," Sam said. "Is everything okay?"

I sighed.

"Oh, Sam, I'm just worried about Mr. Silverman and I guess that's made me cranky."

"That and the fact that she won't be getting any this week," Honey said.

"Uh-oh, let's clean it up, here comes Nathan," I said.

"Did you know that butterflies taste with their feet?" Nathan asked us all.

"No, I did not know that, Nathan," The Goddess said.

"Did you know that elephants are the only animals that can't jump?" Nathan continued.

"Iggy told me they played this game on the way to Disneyland yesterday," Sam said.

Jumping up and down Nathan said, "Did you know that a cat's pee glows under a black light?"

"Speaking of which, I really have to go and check on Mr. Silverman," I said.

"Can I come, too?" Nathan asked.

"Oh, sweetie, Mr. Silverman hasn't been feeling well and he's sleeping so maybe later."

"Silvie's sick? Silvie's sick?" Nathan said, a scared look on his little face.

"Probably not. Just a little under the weather," I said.

The little guy was still sacked out when I got home.

My anxiety was getting the best of me and I decided to give Amanda a call.

She answered on the second ring. I told her Mr. Silverman's symptoms and she said to calm down. It could be nothing or if it was something it appeared I had caught it early.

"Maebeth, drop in at my clinic any time tomorrow morning. You don't need an appointment, just tell the receptionist I'm expecting you."

Amanda went on to tell me that she had met someone and although it was too early to tell where it would go, she was happier than she'd been for a long time. Amanda's longtime partner, Marie, had passed away more than a year ago after a long, painful illness that also jeopardized Amanda's health and caused her practice to suffer. Her new friend, Molly, was a prosecutor with the district attorney's office.

"Well, you and Molly decide when you're both available for dinner. My treat. I can't wait to meet her."

My curiosity was getting the best of me so I asked her how they met.

I could feel Amanda's excitement.

"Believe it or not, we met casually at a gay/lesbian function. A couple of weeks later she called me on a Sunday in a panic because her cat was sick."

"Amanda, my friend, everyone needs a good vet in their life."

I felt better. At least tomorrow Mr. Silverman would be in good hands and I would have some idea of what was going on. I heard a light knock on my back screen door.

"Maebeth, ma'am, is Silvie awake yet?" Nathan said.

"Oh, Nathan sweetheart, come on in. Let's go check on Silvie together and then I was just going to have myself a glass of milk and a chocolate chip cookie. Maybe you could have some, too, and keep me company."

Nathan nodded about seven times and together we walked into the bedroom to check on our little friend.

Mr. Silverman had moved to the bottom of the bed where his favorite faux fur throw was. He opened his eyes and immediately got his motor running as we approached.

Nathan sat down beside him and kissed the top of his large gray head while he stroked him.

"Silvie, you are such a big boy. You are such a big boy. You feel better and you're gonna get a cookie, too."

I smiled.

"In fact, I'm not going to eat my cookie. I'm going to save it for when you get better."

I hoped Henry and Ruth were looking down from heaven and seeing what a fine man this would someday be.

I left the two alone and went out into the kitchen to dry my tears and blow my nose. There was hope for the world yet.

The Lovely Vet

It was another beautiful morning. I let Mr. Silverman in and he headed straight for the bedroom. His appetite was off, but I thought he was looking a little better.

In front of all of our doors was a Bible. Honey must have dropped them off last night. Inside was a Xeroxed note that read:

Ladys at Heve,

Sory i was such a coksuker. Ax aneone an they will sae that is over. God is my sheepherd now. Hope u find it in yer hart to be wid me in grener pastchers.

Catch up widuos later.

Yers in crist an yer frend,

Lenny

What a guy!

Underneath today's dark gray sweatsuit with a zip up hoodie was a white tee with red lettering that read *Humpty Was Pushed.* The run felt good and lately there was added incentive because I couldn't wait to see what was new at Heaven-sent.

I wasn't disappointed for there were flowers planted all around the structure and new gingham curtains in the café. Word had already spread that good things were happening here. There were a least a half dozen cars in the parking lot and a customer pumping gas.

There would be a flyer in the local newspaper promoting the Farmers Market, which was certain to be a success.

When I got back to Heave, I made some breakfast, showered and packed up Mr. Silverman. Iggy and Dennis had gone home. Nathan was off to school and things were getting back to normal, whatever that might be.

Amanda met with us right away. A blood workup was done on my little guy and he was weighed. I hadn't seen any more signs of vomiting. We would have the results later that day.

I mentioned our upcoming Mexican Riviera cruise to Amanda and told her I was worried about leaving Mr. Silverman by himself even though Sam would be around. She told me to definitely plan on the trip and that it would be less stressful for Mr. Silverman if he remained in his own territory. She also said she would stop by and look in on him daily.

What a great heart this woman had!

Later that evening she called to tell me that Mr. Silverman's immune system was compromised and for now she would change his diet and give him weekly Vitamin B shots. There was some swelling in the lymph nodes, but she would wait until I got back before they did any scans.

I felt numb, but it could have been worse. The ladies of Heave had rented a limo for our Sunday trip to Long Beach where our ship would depart for the seven-day cruise. After the cruise, the plan was for me to stay in Malibu with Luke, but I called to cancel because I didn't want to be gone from my little guy for that long.

It was too early to hit the sack so I walked over to Carmen's to see what she was doing. She and Sam were sitting on the floor surrounded by paint and fabric swatches.

"This will be leading edge. It's not modern by any means. Everything will be simple, yet functional," Carmen said before I could ask.

"I'm thinking all the floors should be terra cotta," Sam said. "And we'll grace them with Persian rugs. We should do sleek neutrals and white tints on the walls so that they allow the emphasis to be on some quality pieces and punchy accessories. The contrasts are so important. Maybe a sofa or chair in a rich Italian-worked leather. Look at this picture of a desk that's cantilevered plate glass and stylized chrome. Oh, so elegant, so you, Carmen!"

"Hey, I think this is cool," I said holding up one of their magazines and trying to get into the groove.

"Maebeth, that is a lamp, not a light, and not really even a lamp. Rather we would refer to it as an artistic accessory."

"Bravo, bravo Carmen," Sam said clapping his hands in joy.

"What do you think of some marble in the bathroom?" Carmen said, clearly flushed with all the excitement.

"If you'd excuse me, I think I'll go check, uhhh, whoever's got a light on," I said.

Viva Mexico!

We arrived at Long Beach half in the bag. Charo felt that mimosas would be a good way to start the trip and no one was feeling any pain.

Lucky Charo would have a room to herself while Lily and Julie, The Goddess and Honey, and Carmen and I would share a room.

Being light-headed might not be the smartest way to begin a cruise, but at this point no one had a care in the world.

After boarding we went straight to our rooms to unpack. Waiting for me was a huge basket with fruit, cheeses, crackers and wine. Luke always did things right. For Lily, there was a beautiful "bon voyage" bouquet of calla lilies from Dennis and Iggy. Julie said she'd have a conversation with Moe when she got back.

Next, we headed for the main deck for the mandatory safety session. Carmen had brought along her iPhone and was snapping way. After the session, Charo and Julie split for the casino. Honey and The Goddess were off to check out the ship, while Lily and I found two chaises by the top story swimming pool, where we could look at the view beyond and feel the warmth of the sun. It took some coaxing to get Lily to take the trip which had been booked way before the tragedy. We all convinced her that she needed a change of scenery and that Nathan would have a ball with Sam. Reluctantly, she agreed and now she held my hand and thanked me for prodding her.

"This must be what they mean by waiting to exhale. Why my neck isn't even stiff and by fingers aren't clenched," Lily said.

"Get used to it, sister. We have seven days of this and the only escape is to jump overboard," I said.

"I don't think I ever want to move off this chaise."

"Well, I think we'll have to because we're scheduled for a 6:00 p.m. dinner seating," I said.

"Lawdy, lawdy, I don't have to make any pbj's tonight for school tomorrow."

When everyone was seated for dinner, Julie surveyed the crowd and said, "Not exactly your luxury liner crowd."

"But the gamblin's great," Charo said. I'm up 50 bucks and I'm not even warmed up. Let's chow down and get back to the casino."

Carmen had us all huddle in close so she could take our picture.

Approaching our table was a swarthy, pock-marked young man. "Hello, my name is Pierre. I will be your waiter for the cruise. Upfront, I need to inform you that my livelihood is dependent on the tips I receive at the termination of each voyage. I am at your service."

"Bit of a shitass," Charo said in a stage whisper that hopefully Pierre didn't hear.

Next came course after course with long intervals in between.

"This might not work for me," I announced to my shipmates.

"For God's sake, Maebeth, this is our first night. All this marvelous food. And, I hear they give tours of the kitchen. Charo, would you be up for that?" Carmen asked.

"Sure, Carmen, if the blackjack table is shut down, let's do it," Charo said.

"Well, I'm going to check out tonight's entertainment," Honey said. "Who's coming with me?"

Everyone was up for walking off the meal and checking out the ship activities.

"Oh, here's a little boutique," Julie said. "My God, there's nothing here but Lladros and crap. And, just look at these prices. Jeez."

"Let's go to the casino. We know what's there. I'm feeling lucky," Charo said.

We checked out the swimming pools, spa, beauty shop and gym. There was a pizzeria on the top deck that would afford great daytime views.

Tonight's entertainment was a singer named Carlos Lopez. Word was he was a second cousin of Trini. We decided to stay for a while but being an early riser, I was already nodding off and didn't know if I could stay awake.

We got comfortable in a plushy cushioned banquette and ordered cocktails. There was a tent card on the table announcing an Amateur Night talent contest on the last night of the cruise. First prize was a $1,000.

"I'm in," Honey said.

"You can't whistle up there. They'll know it's not your vulva and you'll be through, end of Desiree," I said.

"No, I'll do my nightclub act."

I nodded.

"Would that be fair?" Lily said. "Aren't you a professional?"

"Well, what about me? I haven't sung in front of an audience for a long time, but I'm sure I can still belt one out," Julie said.

"Why don't you two sing a duet, like the Andrews Sisters?" Charo said.

"There were three of them, and besides, I have my own material," Honey said.

"Yes, we'll each do our own thing," Julie said.

We batted back and forth what they would wear and what song each should sing. Then a comedian came on and told some cruise jokes. Finally, crooner Carlos took the stage. He wasn't bad, but he'd need a lot of luck to make this a career.

I was falling asleep and said I had to go back to the room. Everyone else stayed for dancing, which followed the entertainment.

After a wonderful night's sleep thanks to the rocking of the ship, I headed to the gym. I was determined to stay away from Pierre and the formal dining room as often as I could.

I noted that something strange occurred on cruise ships. All anyone could talk about was the next meal and what they would be having. Maybe it was because there was so much food and nothing else to do, but it got on my nerves.

The gym wasn't busy. It wasn't large, but it was adequate. I hopped on a treadmill and zoned out. Lily and I had scheduled massages for later in the morning.

Puerto Vallarta was to be our first port, followed by Mazatlan and Cabo San Lucas.

We all opted to have High Tea and see what shore excursions might be of interest.

As we steamed into Puerto Vallarta, my first thought was how much I would have liked to have shared this with Luke. The coastline was exquisite—dotted with tropical plants, steep mountains and stunning resorts and villas. The travel brochures said that the area was divided into eight neighborhoods and one of them named "Mismaloya" was the village where John Huston made the movie *Night of the Iguana*, which is said to have changed Puerto Vallarta forever.

We decided to stay together and went over our sightseeing options at the first martini bar we could find. Carmen made sure to take our picture clinking glasses in a toast to good times. According to the brochures, there were beautiful beaches, historic cathedrals, numerous restaurants and galleries, and trendy boutiques.

Julie was passionate in her vote to hit the boutiques.

The Goddess strongly agreed that this was a grand idea and the rest of us just followed along.

An area known as Downtown South had a few shops but the merchandise was disappointing to the black belt shoppers in our group.

"Jesus, just what I need, a freaking sombrero," Julie said.

"Try to get into the culture," Carmen said. "Try on that sombrero and let me get a picture. Here check out these straw bags."

"I wouldn't hit a dead dog in the ass with one of those," Honey said.

"I think they're neat. You can get a lot of stuff into one of those. I'm going to buy one," Charo said, still flush from the $225 she won at the blackjack table.

"We need to get something for Sam," Carmen said. "What do you think of this embroidered white shirt?"

"Doesn't get my vote," I said.

"Yuck," Julie said.

"I don't know, Carmen. That looks a lot like what we bury some of the Mexican men in back home," The Goddess said.

The ship was looking real good to me at the moment. It looked like Elizabeth Taylor and Richard Burton weren't down here for the shopping.

After scouring through a few more shops we found a small original painting of a tiny boat in a beautiful cove.

We all agreed that Sam would like it.

We started back for the ship and hit the same martini bar on the way back. After all, we were on vacation.

I couldn't wait to get into my workout clothes. Lily wanted to check out the library. The Goddess was off for a pedicure, while Charo opted for a nap so she could be ready for tonight's bingo game. Julie and Honey were planning to hit the ice cream shop where they wanted to noodle out their routines for Amateur Night.

After what I hoped would be my last dinner seating with Pierre, who by now we were all calling "Shitass," we decided to go for dancing instructions, which could come in handy for those of us who had trouble staying awake in the evening.

"Slinky would have loved this," Julie said.

Our instructor was a dapper gentleman by the name of Nichy Dalton. He was skilled in the waltz, tango, samba, cha cha—all the classics. He was also available to dance with unescorted ladies later in the evening after the entertainment, which I assumed was once again to be the crooning Carlos.

This was a legit deal in that Mr. Dalton's petite wife, Ginger, accompanied him on all the cruises. They both were skilled dancers and thought that this would be a cool way to see the world during their retirement years. Currently, they were eight months into the Mexican Riviera cruises and Ginger said it was their own *Love in the Time of Cholera*. She added that they seldom got off at ports anymore. She'd seen it all and then some.

The class was fun and Ginger and Carmen hit it off. Both loved cooking, gardening, decorating, not to mention crafts.

Our next port would be Mazatlán and we convinced Ginger to ditch the ship and come along with us on the Las Moras Ranch Tour. There was also a City and Shopping Tour but Julie and The Goddess said we should forget it. I still needed to find something to bring home for Luke.

Men are always a pain to buy for.

Everyone, with the exception of Charo, sat through the entertainment. I was looking forward to the dancing and wasn't disappointed. Mr. Dalton was an equal opportunity dancer finding time for everyone. He steered clear of any controversial subjects like religion and politics and instead laced his comments with "Oh, you're so right," "I couldn't agree with you more," and "You're telling me." Someone should clone this guy.

After a late night the Heave ladies were slow getting started. I hit the gym same as always and by now had sworn completely off the dining room. There were enough other satisfying options on the ship. That, coupled with not having to deal with the little, insipid Shitass, made it worthwhile. The haughty way he said things like Duck ala Orange made me want to shove it someplace personal until he quacked. I think a lot of my nautical rage stemmed from worry over Mr. Silverman.

When I got back to door of my room, there was a posse waiting for me.

"Maebeth, it's Charo. She's gone," Julie said.

"Gone, she's dead?" I said.

"No, no, that's not it," Lily said.

"Where the hell is she?" Honey said.

"We can't find her. We went to pick her up for breakfast and she isn't in her room and the bed hasn't been slept in," The Goddess said.

"Oh God, you read about people having gone missing on these cruises. They never find them," Carmen said.

"Christ, who saw her last?" I asked.

"She was heading off to a bingo game. That's the last time any of us saw her," Lily said.

"Okay, let's get organized. Carmen and I will go talk to the ship's captain. Julie, you go with The Goddess and see if she's already in the dining room. Lily and Honey, see if you can find anyone who was at bingo last night and might have spoken with her."

Everyone scattered. We were to report to each other on the top deck at the swimming pool. Two hours later we convened. The ship's officers were on the alert and conducting a search. No one had any luck other than Honey, who had found a man who said he saw a little old lady leave the bingo game almost as it was getting started. She was with a few young boys and a couple older men.

If we were to make Mazatlán, we needed to find her soon. Just then Carmen spotted a pile of beach towels.

"Look over there," Carmen said.

A bunch of towels were scrunched together on a chaise. It looked like they might be wrapped around a body.

Hearts racing, we tiptoed over and there was Charo, sound asleep, still in last night's red cocktail dress and matching rhinestone necklace and earrings. Her sneakers were off and scattered next to the chaise along with her purse.

I nudged her gently. "Charo, everything okay?"

She opened one eye squinting in the morning sun.

"Where's Sam?" Charo asked. "Where am I?"

"Sam's home, Charo. We're on a cruise, remember?" Lily said.

"Oh, shit, where's my purse?" Charo said.

Julie picked up her purse and handed it to her. Charo came awake quickly as she searched through it throwing Kleenex, candy, her room cardkey, lipstick and a sequined coin purse onto her lap. She unzipped the coin purse and said, "Scared me out of my wits, but it's all here."

Charo had met some fellow passengers at bingo. They were up for a little more action and got a poker game together on the top deck by the pool. Charo nailed them for $973 and celebrated with a few too many glasses of champagne that they had brought with them. Her room was too far away so she decided to doze here and that's all she wrote.

"You scared the shit out of us," Carmen, who rarely swore, said. "And, damn, now is when I need my camera."

"Okay, the trauma is over. Who's going to Mazatlán?" I asked.

"Charo, you might want to skip this and catch up on your sleep," The Goddess said.

"Horsefeathers! Are you nuts? I've got pesos up the ying-yang and I'm going. Just need a quick shower. Here, hand me my runnin' shoes."

"I'll call off the sheriff and meet you all later," I said.

"Don't squeal about the game," Charo said.

Ginger joined us and we were off to our second port. We grabbed an open air cab and I jumped off at the first t-shirt shop. I ran in while the others waited.

The beaches were gorgeous and there were lots of cantinas, boutiques and vendor carts. We said we weren't going to shop, but Lily picked up a donkey-shaped piñata for Nathan, and Julie and The Goddess both purchased some silver jewelry and sandals for Moe and Chris. Charo found a handsome leather jacket for Lester and I spotted in a tiny Gallery, a not inexpensive 19th century retablo of Santa Maria in a richly saturated palette of blue, green, red and gold, and purchased it for Luke. When no one was looking, I also picked up eight 4 x 6-inch seashell picture frames.

We had the entire day ahead of us. Ginger was an excellent tour guide and spoke about the countryside as we headed out to Las Moras Ranch, which proved to be our best decision yet.

This was a working ranch with a gorgeous swimming pool. Julie, The Goddess and Honey immediately went to change into their swimsuits. Charo found a chaise and curled up fast asleep under the warm sun. Ginger, Carmen and I signed up for a 45-minute horseback ride in the surrounding foothills. We saddled up with the help of our guide and Carmen said, "We are the three amigos. Let's ride." Carmen and I had been around horses when we were growing up. She, by far, was the more accomplished equestrian, but I could hold my own. Before we rode off into the sunset, Carmen had our guide take our picture.

After a spicy Mexican poolside lunch, cooled down with margaritas, we wandered throughout the hacienda commenting on the authentic Mexican architecture and massive Spanish Colonial furniture.

Our bus back to the ship stopped in the Golden Zone so we could take one last swing at shopping. I made a quick trip back to the t-shirt shop to pick up my purchase. Julie found a leopard print bathing suit. She also netted a gauzy red dress that she said would work much better with her Amateur Night act.

Money was no object for Charo, who purchased a revealing pink satin robe, trimmed in pink fur, with matching high-heel slippers. The robe was an XL and the shoes were size 11. We didn't want to ask.

Back on the ship, most of us decided to catch a few ZZZs for it had already been a full day and tonight was the big night. Julie and Honey were keeping their routines secret, but I know they already had participated in a few rehearsals. The Goddess was set to do their hair and makeup. Working on people who breathed would be a nice change.

We were seated in the large, comfortable banquettes eagerly anticipating tonight's competition. We all ordered cocktails hoping this would settle our nerves. The first act was an elderly gentleman who played "Spanish Eyes" on the harmonica. Next was a very thin young man, likely in his 30s, who did magic tricks. Then the lights darkened and there was a spotlight on a tuxedoed piano player. He began to play and the light widened to show Julie sprawled across the top of piano in her new red dress. Julie was in her 70s, but she somehow had channeled Michelle Pfeiffer's performance in *The Fabulous Baker Boys* and launched into "Makin' Whoopee" while she squirmed around the piano top batting very smoky eyes, compliments of The Goddess. The crowd went crazy with applause. With all her sighs, moans and groans, you couldn't tell that she hadn't practiced her singing for a long time. The only hitch came at the end of her song when the piano player had to help her off the piano. She slipped and hit her butt on the floor and said, "Oh, crap." She was okay, but it wasn't the ending she had hoped for.

Next, was an overweight middle-aged lady who played the ukulele. I thought she was going to need oxygen before her tune was over. That act was followed by a very young boy, possibly pre-school, lip-syncing to Robert Goulet's "If Ever I Would Leave You." I laughed so hard I thought I would wet my pants, but few others caught the humor and thought I was being rude.

The last act was our very own Honey Dean. Dressed in a sparkling white long sheath that showed a lot of cleavage, Honey presented a medley of tunes including "Girls Just Want to Have Fun," "Heigh-Ho" and "Make Someone Happy." She put her heart and hips into that last number and the crowd was on its feet. Against our advice and her initial promise, she did not sing the songs; she whistled the happy tunes.

A drunk in the back of the room yelled, "Is that you Desiree? I love you."

The judges awarded the $1,000 prize to Honey. Julie came in second and received a basket of spa products.

We were proud of them both, but Julie just had to question Honey's amateur status. "My heavens, Honey, I'm thrilled for you, but it's not like you don't do this for a living and that makes you a professional in my book."

Undaunted, Honey said, "I'm a professional singer, not whistler. Wow, this is going towards my new wheels. What do you think about a van?"

No one commented and instead we decided to dance a few with Nichy and visit with Ginger. Late nights were becoming a way of life. Tomorrow would be our last port and although all of us had a ball, Heave was wonderful to come home to. Heave was more than its inhabitants—it was the concept, the freedom, the beauty of the desert—it was home.

"Hola, Sam," Charo said. We had just set foot in Cabo San Lucas and Charo wanted to tell Sam we'd be home tomorrow. She inquired about Mr. Silverman and Sam said that Amanda had been by and everything seemed fine. Lily was next wanting to know if Nathan was behaving.

"He's right here, Lily," Sam said handing the phone to Nathan.

"Grandma, did you know that dolphins sleep with one eye open?"

"Lawdy, that is very interesting sugar, but have you been a good boy and have you been doin' your homework?"

"Oh, yes, and I get to go to Heaven-sent with Sam and help in the store. And, Mr. Silverman follows me everywhere. And, I'm in the Christmas play at school as one of the wise man who is carrying myrrh. Teacher said there would be room for all of you to come. Do you think Dennis and Iggy would want to come?"

"Why, child, I'll be sure and ask. You know your grandma is missing you so much. It's fun to be on a boat, but it would be even more fun if my little man was with me."

"Did you see any dolphins?"

"Not yet, but I'm sure we will."

"Grandma, did you know that slugs have four noses?"

Lily grinned.

"Wait 'til I tell the girls," Lily said. "You be a good boy and I'll see you tomorrow. Oh, and I have some presents for you."

"Oh, boy," Nathan said.

I had promised myself that I could go a week or so without Luke, but with everyone clocking in and with Mr. Silverman supposedly okay, I couldn't resist. I got Luke's answering machine and told him I was catching the limo tomorrow to Heave and would call as soon as we docked. I begged him not to make the trip to Long Beach and to enjoy his weekend. In some maniac moment, I said, "Buttercup, I love you and miss you."

Cabo San Lucas, located at the tip of the Baja peninsula, was once a tranquil fishing village and now was a mecca for yuppies seeking to capture a romantic lifestyle in their retirement years. Our small boats docked at the beaches, which were littered with vendors selling Mexican handicrafts, silver, ceramics and wood carvings.

We strolled the beach, stopped for a margarita and decided we had had enough and would rather head back to the ship for a siesta. We did rethink sombreros and everyone bought one for themselves and for their family and friends.

That included Moe, Chris, Lester, Brad, Manual, Jose, Sam, Nathan, and of course, Luke.

Our final evening was spent saying goodbye to new acquaintances and getting in a last dance with Nichy. Charo hit the casino, but was under strict instruction from all of us to not give us any more heart attacks.

We exchanged phone numbers with Ginger and invited her to Heave to hang out with some landlubbers for a change. It turned out that Ginger and I had belonged to the same sorority in college and equally were aghast at their exclusionary practices. Lily also had a few derogatory remarks recalling incidents she had witnessed during her years teaching.

"They really like everything vanilla," Lily said. "Maybe that's why those Barbie dolls piss you off so, Maebeth."

It took forever for the ship to dock. We all couldn't wait to disembark and get back to Heave. All of us donned our sombreros and danced down the gangplank arm in arm to the music of mariachis who were welcoming us home. Julie spotted a chauffeur with a discreet sign that read: Heave.

As we waited for our luggage and packages to be loaded, I saw a familiar face with a huge grin.

"Oh, no, it can't be," I said.

There was Luke with his hands on his hips, shaking his head.

"Hola, ladies," Luke said.

My sombrero had slipped down over my eyes as I made a mad dash for his arms, tripped and fell into them.

Luke gently lifted the huge hat from my head, placed it on the ground and stared deeply into my eyes.

"Probably wouldn't be wise to take the rest of your clothes off here, would it?"

I smiled.

"Well, it is pretty warm," I said. "Dammit, Buttercup, I just love it when you don't listen to me. Didn't I tell you not to bother hauling down here. You are a busy man and I have to get home to check on Mr. Silverman."

"What a coincidence," Luke said. "I happened to be heading out that way. Could I interest you in a ride?"

A chorus of "Damn right," "You go, girl" and "I'll go if you don't" filled the air.

Charo ran over to embrace Luke and said she'd whip up something fine for him because he probably was going to be working up an appetite once he got to Heave.

So, I said "no" to the limo and jumped in Luke's Jag.

My luggage and gifts would arrive with the limo.

"Babe, I even missed your t-shirts. What's today's mantra?"

I parted my jacket so he could read *Dedicated to Going Nowhere*. "This kind of fits with my mood today. The trip was fun, but I think New England and you are more my style lately. Actually, a six-pack, an aluminum lawn chair and you beside me in the desert would do it for me."

"Babe, you're talkin' trailer trash. I see you more with champagne, a king-size bed and a suite at the Four Seasons."

"Would you be in the suite?"

"I'd be in the bed."

I babbled on about the ports, Honey's win and the daily food orgies. Luke brought me up to date on a new security job he had obtained from a large corporation. It would involve some travel, the money was good, but the real attraction was that it was a challenge.

"Not dangerous, I hope."

"I'm good at what I do, Babe. The most dangerous thing about the whole gig is telling you that I have to head back to LA first thing tomorrow morning for a flight to Atlanta. Should be gone most of the week."

I nodded.

"So, this is going to be your definition of a quickie?'" I said.

"No, Babe, I plan to take my time with you. That is if there's room for a big welcome for both Mr. Silverman and me."

"You know, you'll always be second."

"Kinda reminds me of a favorite t-shirt slogan I saw years ago," Luke said.

"So, tell me."

"It was *You Can't Be First But You Can Be Next*."

"I like that. I'll have to get one made up with that on it," I said. "Oh, that reminds me. I have some gifts for you."

"I think I'm going to have to break the speed limit if we're going to get all these festivities accomplished before tomorrow morning," Luke said.

Nothing becomes Heave like being away for a while and returning. No hotel suite, ship's cabin or cozy B&B bedroom could ever come close to what we ladies had made for ourselves.

My doors were open, luggage dropped off in the bedroom and awaiting my arrival was the one and only Mr. Silverman. If he was happy to see me, I couldn't tell. Cats. Maybe he was punishing me for being away. He did warm up to me and did look thinner. I hoped it was just my imagination and made a mental note to call Amanda first thing in the morning.

Being as civilized as we are, Luke and I had a glass of wine before we ripped our clothes off. There was never anything routine about our lovemaking. It was always fresh and yet familiar.

It was too early to turn in and we were both hungry. Luke showered and went out to get some carryout Chinese, while I showered and slipped into a comfortable flannel gown.

The food was delicious. Better than anything I had down Mexico way. First, I gave Luke his sombrero. He loved it and said we could now ride horses on the beach together like two caballeros. Still wearing the big blue and silver-trimmed hat, he opened the package containing the retablo and was visibly touched.

"Oh, Maebeth, this is the most magnificent gift I have ever received. 'La Inmaculada,' she is beautiful."

"And one last gift," I said.

Luke opened the package containing a black t-shirt with white letters that read: *Buttercup, you fill me up.*

"Come here," Luke said with a catch in his voice.

Silvie's Sick

Luke had an early invitation to join Charo for another heart-stopping breakfast before he left for LA. I walked him to the door, kissed him goodbye and scooped up Mr. Silverman who was waiting to come in. I placed the little guy on my bed and climbed in beside him. In no time he was purring. We stayed like that for a while and then I covered him and got up to shower.

There was a lot to do since I had been gone for over a week. Groceries, dry cleaning, stacked up mail all needed to be attended to. But first, I wanted to check in with Amanda.

Her office hours started at 8:00 a.m. and I must have been the first business of the day because she came to the phone immediately. After we chatted about the cruise and what she and Molly had been up to the past week, the conversation turned serious.

She had checked in on Mr. Silverman numerous mornings before work. Twice she had found small amounts of vomit. In addition, his appetite was still off and she noted patches of rough hair on his coat. Amanda said she wanted to do a scan and suggested I bring him in today.

I had known in my heart that this time was coming, but I had hoped it was years away. I had lost pets before, but each time was different and at no time was it any easier.

I decided to let the little guy rest. He looked so comfortable and I set off to do a few of the errands. My mind was elsewhere and I almost backed into another car at the lot in the center where I shopped. This wasn't working. Best I go home and take Mr. Silverman to the vet's.

"Maebeth, there is some swelling in the lymph nodes. And, I'm sorry to say we've found some tumors in some of his organs. This is feline lymphoma," Amanda said.

"Oh, my God, what can we do to help him?"

"There are some aggressive treatments, but his immune system is already compromised and I doubt if he could survive them," Amanda said.

Just like Slinky, I thought. She chose to reject treatment and get the most out of the time she had left. I couldn't bear to let Mr. Silverman suffer.

"How much time do you think he has?" I said.

Amanda put her arm around me while I held the little guy in my arms. "I wouldn't let it go too long. He's getting weaker every day. Why don't I give him a shot that will make him more comfortable and you take him home. You don't need to decide this now. Sleep on this and I will call you tomorrow."

I was shaking so hard I wasn't sure I could drive us both home safely. I sat in the car cradling him in my arms and sobbing. Finally, I grabbed a wad of tissues, wiped my eyes and blew my nose. I knew he could sense my grief and didn't want him to suffer because of me.

When we pulled up in front of my unit, Beau and Sue were standing outside my door. I put Mr. Silverman down and the two dogs herded him into my unit. I didn't know what higher power was at work, but these animals had their own language and I marveled at their compassion.

Lily rapped on my door and asked if I'd seen Beau. "He's been hanging around your door all morning."

"Oh, Lily," I cried, falling into her arms. "It's Mr. Silverman. He's very sick and I'm going to have to put him down. Don't ask me how Beau and Sue know, but they were here when I got back from seeing Amanda."

"Sweet Maebeth, sweet Maebeth," Lily said, patting my back and rocking back and forth with me.

"Lily, I'm so embarrassed carrying on like this in light of all you've been through, but it hurts so much."

"Shush, sweet girl, it's all about love and you cry on my shoulder all you want. You are such a special person. You're always there for all of us and I will never forget how you marshalled the troops for Henry and me. You are my very special sister. Now let's see where those 12 paws have headed."

Sure enough they were all in my bedroom. Mr. Silverman had found his favorite spot on my pillow and Beau and Sue respectfully stayed on the floor next to that side of the bed. I covered Mr. Silverman and Lily and I decided that the guard dogs would come out when they felt it was time.

"Lily, did Sam or Nathan say anything about Beau and Sue hanging around here while we were on the cruise?"

"As a matter of fact, Nathan commented that Silvie must be planning a Christmas party with those two because they had been hanging at your front door at lot. I didn't think a thing of it because such strange things often come out of Nathan's mouth lately."

I nodded.

I got on the phone and called Julie. She said that she wondered where Sue had wandered off to and had noticed that she wanted out of the house earlier than usual this morning.

Next, I called Sam and was told that the two dogs had been walking back and forth my front door all the time we'd been gone. Since he had only been at Heave a few months, he didn't realize that that might be unusual behavior. Mr. Silverman had spent most of his days inside my unit but did venture out at night like always.

Lily and I walked outside. I left the front door ajar and soon the two dogs came out. I walked down to Carmen's and like the animals, she had a sixth sense and knew there was something wrong. By now, all the ladies at Heave just "happened" to drop in at Carmen's. There weren't a lot of words spoken, but the deep bond of sisterhood was never stronger. I told them I needed to think about what I was going to do and although I loved them all, I really needed to be alone. Charo looked stricken and asked if I had called Luke. I explained to everyone that he was traveling and I really not only didn't want to burden him, but didn't want to have to worry about his worrying about me.

"Anything you need, we're here," Carmen said.

Mr. Silverman was still sleeping when I returned. He looked angelic and I figured the shot had kicked in. I busied myself dusting, cleaning the fruits and vegetables I had purchased earlier and scrubbing my kitchen floor. Then I washed down all the cabinets and cleaned out the pantry tossing long-expired food. I had not ironed for over a month and decided that would be something that should be taken care of. Also, my windows needed washing and what about giving the bathroom a good scour.

Exhausted, I poured myself a glass of pinot grigio and immediately felt sleepy. It struck me that I had forgotten to eat all day. I made myself a peanut butter sandwich and poured another glass of wine.

Mr. Silverman had gotten up a few times for water and the litter box. He sniffed at his food and refused his favorite treats. When it was time to turn in, I opened the front door, but he declined to leave so I put him back in bed and crawled in next to him. Once again he revved up his little motor and fell asleep in the crook of my neck.

When I woke, the digital clock read 4:18 a.m. My neck was killing me, but my little man was still there. I placed my hand on his back. He was still. I gently extricated myself and he didn't move.

I got out of bed and looked down at him. His beautiful face looked peaceful. Had he waited until I came home to say goodbye? I bent over and kissed him softly between the ears and told him he was the best friend I had ever had and no one would ever take his place. Then I went to my dresser and pulled out a soft pink pashmina shawl that I had been saving for a special occasion. Carefully, I wrapped it around him and left him on the bed.

There were no tears. Some kind of quietness had come over me. I went into the kitchen and sat down with a glass of gingerale hoping it would settle my stomach. Soon it would be light and when it was a more reasonable hour, I would phone Amanda. For now, I wanted to remember Mr. Silverman and all of the wonderful times we had.

My reverie was broken by a scratching at the back screen door. I opened it to find Sue. Julie must have let her out to do her business and she had come over to my unit. I let her in and she walked into the bedroom and lay at the foot of the bed.

At about 8:00 a.m. I phoned Amanda and told her what had happened. She was full of condolences and asked if I wanted cremation. The word jolted me, but I said "yes" and she said she would be over shortly and would pick Mr. Silverman up. I went to the front door to let some fresh air in and there was big Beau, sitting on my doormat. I let him in and he also went directly for the bedroom.

When Amanda arrived, we sat and talked for a few minutes. She had a box with her and said she would handle things from here. I was totally numb as I went in to the bedroom and picked up my little guy. I kissed him again on the forehead and then placed the shawl completely around him, walked out into the living room and handed him to Amanda. Beau and Sue were at my heels.

When everyone had left, I felt empty. God, how I wanted my mother. If I could just have her arms around me one more time, I could get through this.

So Long, Sweet Boy

A week had gone by and Amanda had delivered Mr. Silverman's ashes in a simple cedar box. Lily and I explained to Nathan that Silvie had gone to join Henry and Ruth and would be very happy in heaven. Luke had returned from Atlanta and wanted to be with me, but I assured him I was okay and wanted to be alone a little longer.

I was straightening out a stack of magazines when there was a soft rap at the front door. Through the screen door I saw a large man who looked like he had spent his life outdoors. He said his name was Joseph Martin and he owned a farm down the road. He was looking for a gray cat that he called Sophie. He went on to explain that his wife had passed away five years ago after a long illness. Each night since, he would sit out on his front porch and be greeted by a homeless gray cat. They had a ritual where he would have special treats and Sophie would jump up on his lap to retrieve them. Then, they would sit there and Joseph would tell his friend about all the wonderful times he had spent with his dear wife and their six children. For the past week, Sophie had missed her nocturnal visits and he grew concerned about his old friend.

"Come in, please. May I call you Joseph? My name is Maebeth. Maebeth Caletti."

"Of course, please call me Joseph. I am so sorry to bother you, but I have been asking around and learned that you have a cat that fits Sophie's description. I'm so worried about her. Lately, she hasn't been interested in her treats and looks thinner. And, now she's gone missing and I've been worried about coyotes, speeding cars—you name it."

Taking a picture from an end table, I handed it to Joseph and asked if this was the cat.

"Oh, yes, that's my Sophie."

I was smiling as I explained that Sophie wasn't homeless, female or totally loyal. I also recalled the events of the past week and pointed to the cedar box.

Joseph started to weep. I put my arm around this big stranger's shoulder and together we swapped stories about the cat that led two lives.

"Maebeth, who would believe this story?" Joseph said.

I grinned and patted his arm.

Then I invited Joseph over for the burial which was to take place the next morning at Heave. I also handed him the framed picture and told him I had many more.

"How can a few pounds of whiskers and fur touch one's heart so?" Joseph said wiping his eyes.

"Sophie Silverman was special," I said.

Joseph returned the next morning. The ladies of Heave introduced themselves as we sat out around the pool. Joseph told us how he now leased the fields that he and his ancestors had farmed for many years. Sophie had filled a void for him after his wife, Lois, passed. His children were grown and living all across the country. He said days were long and he hadn't thought how lonely he was until Sophie had disappeared.

Sam asked him if he had been to Heaven-sent.

"The place is looking great," Joseph said. "Best pies I ever tasted. Right now the Farmers Market is a little puny, but it has potential if the owners could get in touch with the right farmers."

"Do you know any of these farmers?" Sam asked.

"Why, sure, I've lived and worked the land in this area all of my life."

Sam explained Heave's connection with Heaven-sent and inquired if Joseph might be interested in managing the Farmers Market. "I could sure use some help," Sam said.

"Why, that sounds swell. I've got lots of ideas."

The two shook hands and then The Goddess and Honey said it was time to start the ceremony. The Goddess had prepared a collage of pictures of Mr. Silverman and placed it on an easel. Sam had dug a small grave in a flower patch in front of The Way of the Cross. Carmen had arranged for a small headstone with the inscription: Mr. *Silverman—loved by all at Heave.*

Honey began singing "Amazing Grace" and we all joined her as I placed the cedar box in the ground. Now all of us were sniffling as Sam filled in the hole and placed some wildflowers on top. Charo asked everyone to stay for pie and coffee. She winked at Joseph and said, "I am heaven-sent to you and want you to take home one of my apple pies."

Even in death, Mr. Silverman was bringing joy to those he touched.

Holidays at Heave

The Christmas season was not a favorite for anyone at Heave. The holidays conjured up lost friends and relatives and more youthful times. All of us at Heave felt the same. We didn't do a formal gift exchange, but remembered each other in our own unique ways. I had prints made of all of us in sombreros disembarking the cruise ship and framed them in the seashell picture frames I had purchased in Mexico.

Dennis and Iggy would be coming to Heave for a few days and then would return to Savannah with Nathan so that he could spend some time with Ruth's parents. Lily was going to cook a holiday meal for Manny and Jose. Sam had finished decorating Carmen's place and, as a holiday gift to me, was expanding my bedroom closet. Possibly, this was a subtle way of saying Luke was here to stay. Honey and Brad were planning a long, luxurious weekend at the Ritz-Carlton Laguna Niguel in Dana Point.

I had gotten over my fear of freeways after a few practice runs into LA with Sam and would be driving to Luke's for the holidays. He wouldn't reveal what he had planned. We hadn't seen each other since before he left for Atlanta and that was weeks ago.

Although I had been emphatic about no gifts, I did order an enlarged picture of the sombrero shot and had all of the ladies at Heave write special greetings for Luke on its wide mat before I had it professionally framed. I also splurged on a first edition of Raymond Chandler's *The Lady in the Lake* and a small diamond earring that I thought would look great on him. I looked forward to his reaction, which I suspected would be one of resistance. Carmen was in her holiday knitting mode so I commissioned her to make a soft orange wool sweater for Miss Daisy. For the Bergmanns, I would bring two of Charo's famous pies.

The Saturday before I was to leave, Charo and I drove over to Heaven-sent to check out the Farmers Market. Already we could see a big improvement with better displays and a wider selection of organic produce. Joseph had also added vendors who, from their canopied booths, sold lemon ice, subway sandwiches, espresso, Danish pastries and Mexican fare.

Amanda had told me about Joyce, a client of hers who was looking for good homes for her cat's most recent litter. Unbeknownst to Joseph, I had arranged for Joyce to bring a few of the kittens to the Farmers Market.

When I spotted her standing at the rear of her SUV, I went over and introduced myself and looked at a box of five of the dearest kittens in an amazing variety of colors and markings.

I went to fetch Joseph and when he saw the contents of the box, he beamed.

"You are allowed no more than two," I said.

"Oh, Maebeth, they are just remarkable. One will do, but they are all wonderful. Oh, look at the gray one with the white on its throat and paws. But then that tabby is cute. I can't decide," Joseph said.

That morning Joseph became the proud parent to both of those kittens. And, he had two Sophies for both were female.

"You have done so much for me," Joseph said, with a catch in his voice.

"You may regret you ever knocked on my door. Now, you're officially a friend of Heave and trust me, you'll never be bored."

"What about a kitten for you, Maebeth?" Joyce said.

"Maybe someday. It's just too soon, but thanks."

I went into Heaven-sent to retrieve Charo. Sam and Carmen had outdone themselves with festive holiday decorations throughout the cafe. Charo was walking from table to table introducing herself as *the* Charo of Charo's Famous Homemade Pies. As she worked the room, there was an Eva Perón quality about her. Those who hadn't had the pleasure of tasting her pies were treated to a small sample. I hated to take her away, but we needed to get back.

The days went quickly and before I knew it I was packed up and on the road to LA. Luke had given me a key to his home and I hadn't been definite about when I'd arrive. The I-10 was a coronary in the making, but something I needed to master and it did get easier as my confidence increased.

Luke was bundled up in a black velour sweatsuit with Miss Daisy next to him on a chaise on the deck. Miss Daisy's tail went into overdrive and Luke greeted me with a warm kiss and relieved me of my luggage. There was a ton more of stuff that needed to brought up from my car. A bottle of champagne chilling in an ice bucket and crackling fireplace were the first things I saw when we entered the the living room.

"Buttercup, this is so damn cozy. It almost puts me in the holiday spirit."

"Let me get you a glass of champagne. Or better yet, you've been driving for hours, let's take our drinks and Miss Daisy and walk on the beach and get the kinks out."

It was a gray December day, but everything around me was warm and welcoming. Malibu was becoming my second home.

We held hands and walked the beach, sipping our champagne and throwing sticks for Miss Daisy along the way. Knowing I enjoyed basketball, Luke had tickets that evening for a Lakers game. I wondered what else he had planned.

Staples Center is always an experience. Just watching some 17,000 fans—not to mention the celebrities—was an event in itself. The Celtics were in town and gave the Lakers a win for Christmas and for a change.

It was a fun evening and a nice contrast to the silence of the desert, although I much preferred the latter. When we got home, Luke got the bedroom fireplace going and then went down to get the rest of the packages and suitcases out of my car.

"I hope this means you're moving in," Luke said as he set the last box down in the dining room and tried to catch his breath.

"That reminds me. I had planned to get you a defibrillator for Christmas what with all those Charo meals you scoff down."

"In about a half hour, let's see who's breathless then."

"Promises, promises."

I poured two snifters of brandy and carried them into the bedroom. Then I showered and put on my favorite, well-worn long flannel blue gown.

"That'd be Vickie's Secret?"

"No, smartass, that'd be I don't want to catch cold. You're just lucky I've decided to skip the Vicks VapoRub tonight. Just thought of something. When we were in Mexico Charo bought the weirdest robe and slippers. Very large size. I need to look into that."

The next morning both of us were up bright and early. We had nothing planned for the day, but wanted to start out with a run on the beach. Today's sweatshirt read: *If I Throw a Stick, Will You Leave.*

Luke took a look and grinned.

"Babe, I hope Miss Daisy can't read. You think that'll throw the neighbors off that we're not an item?"

"I think they probably already expect that I'm your daughter."

The day was overcast and jogging down the beach in the sea air was invigorating. During rest stops I told Luke about the horseback riding we did in Mexico and said I thought that would be great fun on the beach.

After the run, we hopped in Luke's pickup and drove over to the Malibu Country Mart, an area known for its trendy boutiques, bookstore and espresso bar. The crowd was unshaven, sloppily dressed and very artsy-fartsy.

While sipping a cup of hot tea at Malibu Kitchen and nibbling on a bagel, I reached into my pocket and pulled out a small box with a red bow.

"Here, this is for you. Think of it like a hostess gift, or in your case, host."

"How nice. Let's see what we have here. I'm nervous that you're proposing."

What the hell does that mean?

"Dream on, Buttercup."

"What is it?" Luke said, holding the diamond earring in his palm.

"It's an earring. I thought you'd look so hot with one of these."

"Uhhh, I don't think so."

"Oh, come on, what's the problem?"

"First, thanks for thinking of me, but for one thing, I'm not P. Diddy. And, I'm also not light on my feet as you well know. And besides, putting a hole in your ear, well, it's unnatural."

"Okay, of those three objections, which one is your biggest concern?"

"Putting a hole in my ear, hands down."

"You know, you wouldn't have to wear it all the time. You could just have some fun with it. Why look, next door is a jewelry store. Let's see if they do ear piercing."

After a lot of drama, Luke got his ear pierced and was wearing a tiny diamond starter earring. I could tell he was tickled with it, but didn't want to admit it.

"You are so cool, dude. I just might have to notch up my look a little to keep a looker like you interested."

The Bergmanns had invited us over for dinner. I told Lucy that I would bring the dessert. Luke forgot all about the earring and when we arrived, Mel gave him a ribbing while Lucy chastised her husband for being so stodgy.

Mel grilled some salmon while Lucy tossed a Caesar salad and cooked fresh green beans. Everyone raved over Charo's pecan pie. Mel asked what our plans were for the holiday and Luke announced that the two of us would be spending a quiet time at home.

"Love it. This is the first I've heard of this and I am delighted."

I called Carmen to check on things back home. She told me Honey used her cruise winnings and insurance money to purchase Sam's almost-new car, while Sam was buying a van for Heaven-sent and would use that. The Goddess was preparing for a holiday screening of Frank Capra's *It's a Wonderful Life* at the Coachella Valley Cemetery. Joseph was having the time of his life arranging for an antique farm equipment and old truck show at Heaven-sent. Carmen had discovered Lester wearing the lady's robe and slippers while listening to an old Redd Foxx album with Charo.

Back at Luke's, we chucked our shoes and snuggled up on the couch. We were sipping brandy and the fireplace cast off a warm glow. The only sound was that of waves crashing against the shore.

Luke reached into his pocket and placed a tiny aqua Tiffany's box with a white bow in my hand.

"I thought we said no Christmas gifts," I said.

"Think of it as a New Year's present."

I carefully opened the box to find a magnificent square cut ruby ring. I was speechless.

"Thought it would go with those earrings you never take off."

"Oh, Luke, I don't know what to say."

"Babe, let's neither of us speak and you answer this question." With that he pulled off his sweatshirt and underneath was a bright red t-shirt and inscribed in white were the words: *MARRY ME?*

Printed in the United States
By Bookmasters